When You're Confused & Uncertain

Take a lesson from Abraham

When You're Confused & Uncertain

Take a lesson from Abraham

GENE A. GETZ

Regal Books

A Division of GL Publications
Ventura, California, U.S.A.

Rights for publishing this book in other languages are contracted by Gospel Litera-
ture International (GLINT) foundation. GLINT also provides technical help for
the adaptation, translation, and publishing of Bible study resources and books in
scores of languages worldwide. For further information, contact GLINT, Post
Office Box 6688, Ventura, California 93006, U.S.A., or the publisher.

Second Edition, First Printing 1986

Formerly published under the title: *Abraham: Trials & Triumphs*.

Library of Congress Cataloging in Publication Data applied for.

Getz, Gene A.
    When you're confused and uncertain.

    (Biblical renewal series)
    1. Abraham (Biblical patriarch) 2. Patriarchs (Bible)—Biography. 3. Bible.
O.T.—Biography. I. Title. II. Series.
BS580.A3G43   1986   222'.110924   86-477
ISBN 0-8307-1122-8

ACKNOWLEDGMENT

A special word of appreciation to my good friend and colleague, Professor Don Glenn, who teaches in the Department of Semitics and Old Testament at Dallas Theological Seminary. Don took time out of a very busy schedule involving translation work on the *New International Version* of the Old Testament in order to read and evaluate this original manuscript. His suggestions were very helpful. Thanks, Don.

CONTENTS

RENEWAL:
A BIBLICAL PERSPECTIVE

This study of the life of Abraham is another book in the Biblical Renewal Series. Renewal is the essence of dynamic Christianity and the basis on which Christians, both in a corporate or Body sense and as individual believers, can determine the will of God. Paul made this clear when he wrote to the Roman Christians—"be transformed by the renewing of your mind. Then," he continued, "you will be able to test and approve what God's will is" (Rom. 12:2). Here Paul is talking about renewal in both a personal and a corporate sense. In other words, Paul is asking these Christians as a Body of believers to develop the mind of Christ through corporate renewal.

Personal renewal will not happen as God intended it unless it happens in the context of corporate renewal. On the other hand, corporate renewal will not happen as God intended without personal renewal. Both are necessary.

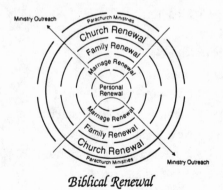

Biblical Renewal

The larger circle represents Church Renewal. This is the most comprehensive concept in the New Testament. However, every local *church* is made up of smaller self-contained, but interrelated units. The *family* in Scripture emerges as the church in miniature. In turn, the family is made up of an even smaller social unit—*marriage*. The third inner circle represents *personal* renewal, which is inseparably linked to all of the other basic units. Marriage is made up of two separate individuals who become one. The family is made up of parents and children who are also to reflect the mind of Christ. And the church is made up of not only individual Christians, but couples and families.

Though all of these social units are interrelated, biblical renewal can begin within any specific social unit. But wherever it begins—in the church, families, marriages or individuals—the process immediately touches all the other social units. And one thing is certain: All that God says is consistent and harmonious. He does not have one set of principles for the church and another set for the family, another for husbands and wives, and another for individual Christians. For example, the principles God outlines for local church elders, fathers and husbands, regarding their role as leaders, are interrelated and consistent. If they are not, we can be sure that we have not interpreted God's plan accurately.

The Biblical Renewal Series is an expanding library of books by Gene Getz designed to provide supportive help in moving toward renewal. Each of these books fits into one of the circles described above and will provoke thought, provide interaction and tangible steps toward growth. You will find a detailed listing of the Biblical Renewal Series titles at the back of this book.

INTRODUCTION

"CONSIDER ABRAHAM!"

Welcome to an exciting story!

In this book I introduce you to an unusual personality —Abraham! Together we'll look at his strengths and his weaknesses, his successes and his failures—his trials and his triumphs. And together we'll learn some profound principles that will guide us in discovering and doing God's will.

Paul penned the words "Consider Abraham," in his letter to the Galatian Christians (Gal. 3:6, *NIV*). And with these words, this first-century apostle was saying that Abraham stands out as one of the greatest Old Testament examples for New Testament Christians. In the midst of other Old Testament greats, Abraham emerges as a man who desired more than anything else to discover and to do God's will.

But Abraham was also a man who suffered all of the ambivalent feelings and mixed emotions that every human experiences—even the twentieth-century Christian. Though his great desire was to obey God, he sometimes disobeyed. He wanted to trust God, yet at times he doubted. Sometimes he stepped out boldly by faith; at other times he drew back in fear. His motives were usually right, but sometimes he used wrong methods. On one occasion he made a mistake so serious that it affected the course of human history. And though Sarah, his wife, was generally very loyal to him, at times she made it very difficult for Abraham to obey God completely.

Yes, Abraham stands out in Scripture as a normal human being. He made mistakes like all of us. But his direction was always "one way." His eyes were on God —and Jesus Christ! This world was not his real home. He passed one of the greatest tests ever experienced by man, and his reputation in the pagan world was beyond reproach. In perspective, his pilgrimage on earth stands out dramatically as a dynamic example to all peoples of the earth. Even with limited knowledge about God and His ways, Abraham discovered God's will and desired to walk in it.

From Abraham's life story emerges dynamic principles that will assist every Christian living in the world today to discover and to do God's will. His Old Testament walk is dramatically alive with New Testament truth. He lived in a culture far removed from ours, yet his basic struggles and victories are alive with supracultural lessons. Though he lived thousands of years ago, he still speaks authoritatively to every twentieth-century child of God.

1

ABRAHAM'S CALL

But don't forget this, dear friends, that a day or a thousand years from now is like tomorrow to the Lord. He isn't really being slow about his promised return, even though it sometimes seems that way. But he is waiting, for the good reason that he is not willing that any should perish, and he is giving more time for sinners to repent.
2 Peter 3:8,9 TLB

Next to Jesus Christ, Abraham is no doubt the most significant man mentioned in the Bible! True, Moses stands out as the greatest prophet in Israel (Deut. 34: 10). But if it were not for Abraham, there would have been no nation for Moses to lead! In fact, if God had not chosen Abraham out of the degenerate and pagan community in which he lived there may have been no Saviour of the world, for it was from Abraham's seed that Jesus Christ came to bless all nations.

Abraham's prominence in God's overall plan for mankind is evident from the titles used to describe him, the amount of space used to record the events of his life and the way he is cited in the New Testament. On several occasions he is called the "friend of God" (2 Chron.

20:7; Isa. 41:8; Jas. 2:23)—an honorable title indeed! Frequently the Scripture writers refer to "the God of Abraham" (how would you like your name to be substituted for Abraham's and recorded in the Bible?). And more than 12 chapters in the book of Genesis are devoted to describing his life.

In the New Testament, Abraham is referred to in four significant letters—Romans 4, Galatians 3, Hebrews 7 and James 2. And in most of these references his life is used to illustrate how man can be saved. All this demonstrates how significant the man Abraham really was!

GENESIS: BOOK OF BEGINNINGS

The story of Abraham begins in Genesis 12. In many respects this is where the main story of the Bible begins. What precedes appears as history compressed. Briefly and succinctly we see the creation of the universe, the creation of man and the origin of sin (Gen. 1–3). We read about the first murder, when Cain killed his brother Abel (Gen. 4). We then see the rapid multiplication and spread of violence and wickedness, resulting in the flood —God's judgment on a sin-sick society (Gen. 6–8). And, because "Noah was a righteous man," a man who "walked with God," he "found favor in the eyes of the Lord" and was preserved, along with his family (Gen. 6:8,9).

After the flood mankind again multiplied on the earth and, true to form, soon turned away from the God of heaven. In some respects, the deterioration became even greater than before the flood. Paul's description of human degeneracy in Romans 1 probably recounts the awfulness of sin that existed in the world when God first appeared to Abraham.

"For even though they knew God," wrote Paul, "they did not honor Him as God, or give thanks; but they became futile in their speculations, and their foolish

13

heart was darkened." They soon "exchanged the glory of the incorruptible God for the image in the form of corruptible man and of birds and four-footed animals and crawling creatures" (Rom. 1:21,23).

The result of this toboggan slide of sin was devastating. In rapid succession Paul records three times the most tragic statement in the whole Bible—*God gave man over to do what he wanted to do!*

From man's perspective Paul's account reflects an X-rated society! From God's perspective it spells judgment and eternal separation from God.

First, "*God gave them over in the lusts of their hearts to impurity,* that their bodies might be dishonored among them. For they exchanged the truth of God for a lie, and worshiped and served the creature rather than the Creator, who is blessed forever" (Rom. 1:24,25, italics added).

Second, "*God gave them over to degrading passions;* for their women exchanged the natural function for that which is unnatural, and in the same way the men abandoned the natural function of the woman and burned in their desire towards one another, men with men committing indecent acts and receiving in their own persons the due penalty of their error" (1:26,27, italics added).

Third, "*God gave them over to a depraved mind,* to do those things which are not proper, being filled with all unrighteousness, wickedness, greed, malice; full of envy, murder, strife, deceit, malice; they are gossips, slanderers, haters of God, insolent, arrogant, boastful, inventors of evil, disobedient to parents, without understanding, untrustworthy, unloving, unmerciful" (1:28–31, italics added).

What a tragedy! When God purified and cleansed the earth from sin by means of the flood and gave man another chance to walk with Him, man once again turned his back on God and went his own sinful way!

But God is a God of love! Even in judgment, He was loving mankind, giving him another chance.

Remember! Though God hates man's sin, He still loves all men. So, in the midst of this human decadence that once again permeated the earth, God began to fulfill a marvelous plan to provide redemption for all mankind. And to implement this plan He chose one man, Abraham, through whom He would bless all nations—in spite of their resentment and hostility toward Him. God was going to give man another chance.

GOD'S CHOICE OF ABRAHAM
(Gen. 12:1)

"Now the Lord said to *Abram* . . ." Abraham was first called *Abram*, which means "exalted father." Later when a promise of numerous progeny was renewed to him by God, he was called *Abraham*, which means "father of a multitude."

God's choice of Abraham was sovereign! Why, out of other possible candidates, He decided to choose Abraham, we do not know. But we do know from Noah's example (Gen. 6:8,9) that when God deals with men, He begins His acts of mercy by communicating with one whose heart is tender toward Him. And, tradition classifies Abraham as such a man. His father, Terah, worshiped idols (Josh. 24:2), yet Abraham rebelled against the idolatry that surrounded him—even in his own home.

But no matter what Abraham's attitude or life-style, Scripture makes it clear that God sovereignly chose Abraham. It was by God's grace that Abraham became the father of nations. And it was because of Abraham's response of faith that he became righteous in God's sight. "For if Abraham was justified by works," wrote Paul, "he has something to boast about; but not before God. For what does the Scripture say? 'And Abraham

15

believed God, and it was reckoned to him as righteousness' " (Rom. 4:2,3).

Isn't this favoritism?

Some people are troubled by the fact that God chose Abraham. They accuse God of favoritism. They don't understand, of course, that all men were lost at this time, and by choice. As Paul stated, again in Romans, "There is none righteous, not even one; there is none who understands, there is none who seeks for God" (Rom. 3:10,11). This statement, generally true of all mankind in all ages, was particularly true when God reached out to Abraham.

God's "particularism" in this instance was a means to make salvation a universal possibility for every man. This was another act of God's mercy—an act of reaching out to sinful humanity. Through Abraham, God was going to make salvation available to the world.

Why didn't God choose another method?

Though God is all-powerful it would be contrary to His holy nature to suddenly pardon all men in spite of their sin and rebellion. He simply could not do it! He chose a process leading to the one final and great sacrifice—the sacrifice of His Son! And He also chose a process that would, because of His patience, long-suffering and grace, *take time* to get His message to man—a message that would come through loud and clear.

Why is the time factor important in God's plan?

One thing is clear about God's judgment on mankind. He does not do things quickly, nor does He act without warnings. Before He destroyed the world with the flood, He had Noah spend 120 years building an ark and preaching about the judgment to come (1 Pet. 3:20; 2 Pet. 2:5).

But this time God decided to use another method—one that would last not just 120 years, but, to date, nearly 4000 years! Step by step He was going to unfold the plan, using a variety of approaches to try and warn man of the judgment to come. In essence that plan is outlined in Genesis 12:1-3. And it began with God's choice of Abraham.

GOD'S COMMAND TO ABRAHAM
(Gen. 12:1)

"Go forth from your country, and from your relatives and from your father's house, to the land which I will show you" (12:1).

Abraham lived in an ancient city called Ur. Nearly 4000 years ago, when God first appeared to Abraham, Ur was one of the most important cities in the world. It was a busy commercial center located in the country of Mesopotamia on the Persian Gulf and bordered by the Euphrates River.

The city covered about four square miles and had a population of about 300,000 people. History records, and archaeology confirms, that many of these people were highly educated. They were proficient in mathematics, astronomy, weaving and engraving. Furthermore they preserved their ideas by writing on clay tablets, which have been invaluable to archaeologists in reconstructing the social and religious life of these people.

Like the rest of the world, Ur was polytheistic. The people worshiped many gods, particularly nature gods. But in the center of Ur was a large worship center or temple called a ziggurat. It was here that the people worshiped their chief deity, a moon god called Nanna.

Abraham no doubt lived with his family outside of the city of Ur. Terah, Abraham's father, was a shepherd who had settled in the rich pasturelands surrounding the city.

But the religious influence of the culture had penetrated this family. They too had become idolators.

It was in the midst of this idolatrous and rather comfortable existence that God appeared to Abraham and gave him a command—the command to leave his country, to break away from his relatives and even to depart from his father's house. And with this command God made Abraham a promise.

GOD'S COVENANT WITH ABRAHAM (Gen. 12:1–3)

"Go . . . to the land which I will show you; and I will make you a great nation, and I will bless you, and make your name great; and so you shall be a blessing; and I will bless those who bless you, and the one who curses you I will curse. And in you all the families of the earth shall be blessed" (12:1–3).

God unconditionally promised Abraham three things—a *land*, a *seed*, a *blessing!* The *land* was Canaan. The *seed* refers to becoming a great nation. The *blessing*, though it would unfold throughout Abraham's life and the lives of those who would live after him, would begin its grand culmination with the birth of Jesus Christ. For Christ was the Saviour of the world—not just of Israel!

Again, God did not choose *Abraham* in an act of favoritism but rather to use him as a channel through whom He would reach the world with the message of salvation. For, from Abraham was to come the nation Israel, whose people would be God's chosen people. Also, God did not choose *Israel* because He was showing favoritism. Rather, He chose this nation to be the mediator between God and the other nations of the world; a nation through whom God would reveal Himself, not only as the God of Abraham, Isaac and Jacob, but the God of all nations. Israel was to be a divine visual aid to show all people that God exists, that He is reaching out to sinful mankind, that He wants all to turn from their sins to be saved.

Dr. George Peters in his *Biblical Theology of Missions* speaks to this point directly: "Israel's history is not a history of arbitrary election, of favoritism, of narrow particularism and nationalism. It is an act of sovereign and gracious election to preserve the race and the temporal and eternal destiny of mankind."[1]

Thus the Abrahamic Covenant forms a divine outline for understanding the rest of redemptive history. The three words in this contract—*land, seed,* and *blessing*—become key words that help unlock the rest of the Bible.

WHAT OF TODAY?

Today we look *back* to the life, death and resurrection of Jesus Christ—the One who would make available a blessing for all families of the earth. Today we are those who are "blessed with Abraham, the believer" (Gal. 3:9). Today we are participants in God's marvelous grace—for if God had not reached down that day and called Abraham, the world would have continued on a collision course that would have led to total destruction, eternal judgment and separation from God.

Perhaps one of the most significant lessons we can learn from this introductory study on the life of Abraham is that God is a merciful and loving God who is reaching out to mankind. He *wants* us to know His will. When the whole world was lost and in a state of active rebellion against God, He sovereignly chose one man who would be an initial part of a redemptive plan that would affect the world in centuries to come.

God's redemptive plan is still unfolding! Though the descendants of Abraham failed God many times and turned from His divine purpose, God's mercy continued. His unconditional promise to Abraham could not be broken. Because of God's grace, the world has continued for nearly 4000 years. God's message of salvation has been heralded continually—at times weak and almost inaudible, but never stifled.

For the first 2000 years God spoke to the world through the nation Israel. During the second 2000 years God has been speaking to the world through the Church —the body of Christ. And some day—perhaps soon— God will once again pick up His program with Israel and literally fulfill the Abrahamic Covenant, providing them with an eternal land, an eternal kingdom and an eternal Saviour.

There are many today who do not understand God's program. They do not understand His will, nor do they understand His grace and patience! Those who watched the building of the ark and rejected Noah's preaching, never knew "the patience of God" that "kept waiting in the days of Noah" (1 Pet. 3:20). Just so, there are those today who are rejecting God's loving invitation.

Peter spoke directly to this issue in his second letter: "Know this first of all, that in the last days mockers will come with their mocking, following after their own lusts, and saying, 'Where is the promise of His coming? For ever since the fathers fell asleep, all continues just as it was from the beginning of creation.' . . . But do not let this one fact escape your notice, beloved, that *with the Lord one day is as a thousand years, and a thousand years is as one day.* The Lord is not slow about His promise, as some count slowness, but is patient toward you, not wishing for any to perish but for all to come to repentance" (2 Pet. 3:3,4,8,9, italics added).

LIFE RESPONSE
· What is your personal relationship with Jesus Christ? Are you ready to meet Him, should you die or should He suddenly appear the second time? Don't reject His love, His patience, His grace!

Some day He *will* come—and then it will be too late! The door of salvation, like the door of the ark, will be closed. God will then turn His face away from those who have rejected Him. And the Bible says, "It is a terrifying thing to fall into the hands of the living God" (Heb. 10:31).

But His grace at this moment is still available! Receive Him today. Accept His gift of salvation. This prayer will help you. Pray it meaningfully by writing your name in the blanks provided.

"Father, I thank you for sending Jesus Christ to be my personal Saviour from sin. And I, _____ _____, confess that I am a sinner—that I have fallen short of your perfect standard. And I thank you that just as you called Abraham out of a pagan world, you are also calling me. And I, _____ _____, now receive Jesus Christ as my Saviour from sin. I believe He died for me personally. Thank you for coming into my life and making me a Christian."

FAMILY OR GROUP PROJECT

Read together Hebrews 11:8–12. Use this passage as a springboard to review this message on Abraham. Have each member of the family share the time when they responded to God's call and received Jesus Christ as his personal Saviour. End the study with a time of family communion, breaking the bread and drinking together the cup in order to remember the Lord's death on the cross.

Footnote

1. George Peters, *Biblical Theology of Missions* (Chicago: Moody Press, 1972), p. 96.

2

ABRAHAM'S OBEDIENCE

*I have loved you even as the Father has loved me. Live
within my love. When you obey me you are living in my
love, just as I obey my Father and live in his love.*

John 15:9,10 TLB

Think of it! For nearly 60 years Abraham had grown
up and lived in a community of people who bowed down
to the gods of nature. Even his own father participated
in idolatrous worship. And all of a sudden God appeared
to him.

What an exciting moment! Abraham must have responded with awe and astonishment.

How all this transpired we do not know. But one thing
is clear. God did not leave room for Abraham to question seriously the reality of this experience. God not
only spoke to Abraham (Gen. 12:1), but also visibly
appeared to him (Acts 7:2).

And God's message was convincing. No man in his
right mind would leave his country, his relatives and his
immediate family to head off for an unknown destina-
tion without being utterly convinced of the rightness of
his decision. The insecurities surrounding such a significant decision must have eventually been dissolved
through Abraham's direct encounter with the God of

heaven. Thus we read: "By faith Abraham, when he was called, obeyed by going out to a place which he was to receive for an inheritance; and he went out, not knowing where he was going" (Heb. 11:8).

ABRAHAM LEAVES FOR HARAN
(Gen. 11:31; Acts 7:2–4)

On the surface it may appear that Abraham's decision to obey God was without difficulties and inward struggles. But a careful study of Scripture, combined with an understanding of human nature, makes it obvious that Abraham experienced inward turmoil.

God called Abraham while he still lived in Ur. "The God of glory appeared to our father Abraham when he was in Mesopotamia, before he lived in Haran" (Acts 7:2). And God made it clear that Abraham was to leave his land, his relatives and his father's house. He was to make a complete break with his idolatrous environment.

But Abraham was only partly obedient, for he never really separated himself from his relatives. For some unknown reason, Abraham left Ur with his father Terah and his nephew Lot. There is biblical evidence that his brother Nahor may also have journeyed with them; though it is possible that Nahor and his family moved to Haran later (Gen. 11:29; 22:20–23; 24:10; 27:43).

So we read: "And Terah took Abram his son, and Lot the son of Haran, his grandson, and Sarai his daughter-in-law, his son Abram's wife; and they went out together from Ur of the Chaldeans . . . as far as Haran, and settled there" (Gen. 11:31).

Scholars calculate that, after leaving Ur, Abraham resided in Haran approximately another 15 years before finally journeying on with his relatives into the land of promise. He delayed in making the complete transition, and this disobedience eventually caused him a great deal of stress, inward pain and outward trouble.

There is a slight clue in the Genesis 11:31 account that may help us to understand what actually transpired after God had called Abraham to leave Ur. Note that this verse states that "Terah took Abram ... and they went out together ... to enter the land of Canaan."

For some reason Terah appears to be in the driver's seat. Evidently he decided to go to this new land with Abraham. Why, we can only speculate.

Let's imagine what may have happened. In today's idiom their conversation could have gone like this:

ABRAM: Dad, you're not going to believe this! You had better sit down!

TERAH: Oh really, son, what happened?

ABRAM: Are you sure you can handle this?

TERAH: Handle what? Make sense, son! What's on your mind?

ABRAM: Well, dad, you know I have been telling you that worshiping idols is a waste of time. It's ... well ... primitive! Remember that I told you that there just has to be someone—someone greater than all of the gods that are worshiped in Ur. Well, I *know* there is now!

TERAH: (Very startled) You what?

ABRAM: I *know* there is a God greater than all gods! I have seen Him! He talked with me!

TERAH: Abram, (Long pause, then soberly) I told you to stay out of the wine-cellar. Right?

ABRAM: Yes, dad. But I haven't been drinking. It's true. I've seen Him and I've *heard* Him!

TERAH: (Somewhat convinced) You're really serious aren't you? You say you've seen Him and heard Him?

ABRAM: Yes, dad, I saw Him in a glorious manifestation! I could just make out an outline of His person, but I heard His voice, clearly, just as

24

clearly as I'm hearing yours right now!

TERAH: Well, what in the world did He say?

ABRAM: Well, it may sound strange, but He told me to pack up and leave Ur.

TERAH: To what?

ABRAM: To leave Ur, and the whole land, and—(Pause)

TERAH: And what, Abram?

ABRAM: To (Pause and very solemnly) . . . to leave you, too, dad. To leave you, my brothers, cousins— *all* my relatives!

TERAH: Nonsense! You *have* been drinking!

ABRAM: No, dad, it's true! And it's real. It was no dream. I've got to go.

TERAH: Go where?

ABRAM: To a land He's going to show me!

TERAH: To a land He's going to show you? You mean He didn't tell you exactly where it is? Oh, Abram—if you aren't drunk, you're sick!

ABRAM: I'm not sick, dad! And I'm not drunk!

TERAH: Well, confound it! Didn't He give you any clue as to where in the world He wanted you to go?

ABRAM: Well, a land He called Canaan, somewhere in the West! And what's more, God promised that He would make me a great nation, and eventually through me all families of the earth would be blessed.

(Several days later, after Abraham had convinced his father that this experience was real):

TERAH: Son—you're not going alone! This "God" you speak of must have something very special for you, and I'm not going to miss it. I have always wanted to be something other than a shepherd. I'm going with you. And we're taking Lot with us, too—after all, I promised your brother before he died that I would take good care of his son. So, let's start packing!

25

This little story of course only illustrates what may have happened. But it is evident that Abraham's father became the leader when they left Ur. This, of course, was in direct violation of God's command. Evidently Abraham was unable to make the complete break with his father, so they started out together—under his father's leadership. Abraham took Sarah, his wife, and—together with his father and his nephew, Lot—they began the long trip along the Euphrates River, heading for Haran. And significantly, when they arrived in Haran, a city just as idolatrous as Ur—and *still* in the land of Mesopotamia—they "settled there" (Gen. 11:31). And there they stayed for approximately 15 years.

ABRAHAM LEAVES FOR CANAAN (Gen. 12;4,5)

God had a plan for Abraham! But while Abraham was close to his father, experiencing the security of family ties and support, he found it easy to forget God's call. Still, even though Abraham was having difficulty in making the complete break, God patiently waited.

Eventually Terah died. Possibly God had to take Terah out of Abraham's life before he could turn his eyes once again on God's great plan and will for his life. One thing is clear: When his father passed away, Abraham once again remembered God's call.

There is a difference of opinion about the place where Abraham received his call. Some believe it was in Haran after he had migrated to the city with his father. But the whole of Scripture does not seem to affirm this idea. Both the Genesis account (Gen. 11:31) and the New Testament account (Acts 7:2–4) indicate that Abraham received his call at Ur. The sequence in Genesis 11:31 to 12:4 becomes very clear if the opening line in Genesis 12:1 is translated: "Now the Lord *had said* to Abram." This is a permissible translation.

"So Abram went forth as the Lord had spoken to him;

and Lot went with him. Now Abram was seventy-five years old when he departed from Haran" (Gen. 12:4).

We now see Abraham's faith coming into full fruition. His previous trip from Ur to Haran, with his father, was a rather secure maneuver. After all, he had maintained his close family ties. Furthermore, they were heading for a familiar city. Culturally, religiously, and in most every way, there was little change in their environment.

And the trip from Ur to Haran was not difficult. In some ways it was like taking a superhighway rather than a cross-country trail. Pastureland was plentiful in which to graze their flocks—a beautiful expanse of land made fertile and lush by waters of the Euphrates River.

Perhaps the closer they came to Haran the more Abraham was tempted to forget about God's call. It may be that his pagan father, whom God knew would have a negative influence on Abraham, began to play on Abraham's sympathy. "I'm getting old, son. Let's forget this whole idea! Let's stay in Haran."

Whatever the reason they had settled in Haran. But when Terah died, God's call once again dominated Abraham's thoughts.

Now the true test of faith! God was leading Abraham southwest, heading out to a place he had never been before. And it meant crossing the burning desert.

Imagine the negative advice he must have received from the relatives he left behind in Haran:

"You're crazy, Abraham!"

"You're out of your mind!"

"There's nothing but a desert out there!"

"You and your wife and servants will all die in that wasteland!"

Knowing something of Sarah's temperament from other scriptural accounts, and particularly at this stage in her spiritual development—plus the security needs of women in general, it doesn't take too much imagination to reconstruct what could have transpired between this man and wife. Many times Abraham must have faced Sarah's numerous moods, alternating between weeping and screaming. It's one thing to face unhappy relatives but still another to face an unhappy wife!

But God *had* to be first! Abraham had no choice if he wanted to carry out God's will.

And obey he did. F.B. Meyer, in his book on Abraham, captures this scene graphically: "And so the caravan started forth. The camels, heavily laden, attended by their drivers. The vast flocks mingling their bleatings with their drivers' cries. The demonstrative sorrow of eastern women mingling with the grave farewells of the men. The forebodings in many hearts of imminent danger and prospective disaster. Sarah may have even been broken down with bitter regrets."[1]

At this point it would have been easy for Abraham to give up the idea—to remain in Haran. But he didn't. He "faltered not. He staggered not through unbelief. He 'knew whom he had believed, and was persuaded that He was able to keep that which he had committed to Him against that day.' He was fully persuaded that what God had promised, He was able also to perform."[2]

ABRAHAM ARRIVES IN CANAAN (Gen. 12:5–9)

Numerous days passed after leaving Haran. There was nothing but monotonous wasteland, as far as the eye could see. There was little vegetation, and water was dispensed sparingly.

Tradition records that they eventually arrived in a beautiful oasis, now called Damascus. In fact, a small village near this city is still called by Abraham's name. And Josephus records that a suburb of Damascus in his day was identified as the "habitation of Abraham."

But Abraham did not stay there. He had learned his lesson well. How easy it would have been to settle down, to stay in this place permanently—or even to turn back. How tempting for Abraham to rationalize and convince himself that he had "obeyed sufficiently."

But God had called Abraham to Canaan. And Abraham kept his eyes on this goal. He had been temporarily sidetracked before by his dearest and closest relative—his own father. But not now! Abraham continued his journey and "thus they came to the land of Canaan" (Gen. 12:5).

God honored Abraham's faith and obedience as He always does. Once this man arrived at the place where God had led him, the Lord once again appeared to him and confirmed His divine promise: "To your descendants I will give this land" (12:7).

This appearance represents the first account of any direct revelation to Abraham since God's initial encounter with him in Ur a number of years before. Thus it seems that God was waiting for full obedience to His will before He gave Abraham the reassurance he so desperately needed.

Abraham had now made the complete transition from an idolatrous environment to worshiping the one and only true God. The most important evidence of Abraham's complete commitment to God stands out clearly in the scriptural records. Twice we read in the space of two verses that Abraham, after he had arrived in the land, built an altar to the Lord (12:7,8). In this way he began to bear witness to his new pagan neighbors that he and his family were different. Their sacrifice and worship were not made to some idol of wood or stone, but to the one and only invisible God—Creator of the heavens and earth.

SOME DYNAMIC LESSONS

There are some powerful lessons that emerge from this study.

1. *God is patient with mankind. He understands our weaknesses, our struggles, our problems!*

This is evident from God's dealings with Abraham. He knew it was a difficult decision for Abraham to leave his homeland, his relatives, his family. So, God was patient with him during the transition, even though He wanted immediate obedience and knew that it would be better for Abraham in the long run to make a quick and clean break. But God often lets us learn the hard way, without forcing us to do His perfect will, even though he knows His way is best.

Knowing that God is patient with mankind can lead to rationalization. Therefore, we must look at the second dynamic lesson from this Old Testament story.

2. *God will not and cannot be manipulated. We will always pay the price for disobedience—even though it is partial obedience.*

Even though Abraham was moving in the general direction of Canaan, he still had not obeyed God's direct and specific command. He was still under the influence of his pagan father, which resulted in delayed obedience. So God eventually removed his father from the scene, freeing Abraham to do His perfect will. Furthermore, God did not speak to Abraham again and confirm His promise to him until he actually arrived in the land of Canaan—until he had obeyed God specifically.

Oftentimes we may wonder why God doesn't seem to be real to us, why He seems far removed. Sometimes—not always—it's because we are trying to manipulate Him, to expect God to guide us and comfort us, even though we are living in a state of disobedience.

The solution, of course, is to confess our sins and to once again be on our way "toward Canaan." Then when we get there, God will honor our obedience. He has promised to never leave us nor forsake us. He is *always* there. The problem is we are not always close to Him.

3. *The fact that we have not obeyed God completely in the past does not mean that we cannot change the situation in the present.*

True, some decisions or actions out of the will of God can be pretty disastrous—for example, marrying a non-Christian, a direct violation of God's will (2 Cor. 6:14). It is virtually impossible to correct this kind of mistake other than by divorce, which in most cases leads us to violate God's will a second time. We can still make the best of the situation by obeying God's commands, even in the midst of the problem where we cannot start over.

But most decisions we make out of God's will are not as complicated as the one that results in a bad marriage. It is never too late to start obeying God. Remember, Abraham was 75 years old when he left Haran.

4. *We must understand how to determine God's will for us today. We cannot expect God to speak directly to us as He did to Abraham. What we must remember is that He has already spoken—through His Word.*

Many Christians make the mistake of expecting God to duplicate in their own lives the same pattern and method He used to reveal His will to Abraham. We do this because we don't understand that God works in different ways at different times in history.

In this Old Testament story, Abraham represents an important beginning point in God's revelation to man. Prior to the written revelation of God which we have in the Bible, God actually appeared to certain men and spoke to them directly. Today we have the divine record of those events, plus numerous directives that specifically spell out His will for us. We need not wait for God to speak. He has already spoken.

It is dangerous for us as Christians to rely on our own experiences in determining God's will. Many impressions that we feel are coming from God may be coming from our own selfish desires—or even from Satan. So we must always evaluate our decisions in light of the Scriptures. We must always ask: What has God *already* said?

LIFE RESPONSE

Are you having difficulty obeying God? You already know what He says you must do. Are you violating His will, either totally or partially? If you are, decide today that you are moving on toward "Canaan." Turn your back on those who may be telling you you're crazy, and turn your eyes on Jesus. Don't be afraid to face the uncertainty of the future—even the "burning desert." God will honor your decision. "Build an altar" today and worship the God of heaven.

Be specific. Write out your decision. And then pray that God will help you carry it out.

Today I have decided to obey God's Word. This means I *must* and *will* _____

_____

Signed:_____

FAMILY OR GROUP PROJECT

Read together Romans 12:1,2. Answer the following questions:

1. What does it mean to present our bodies to God, a living and holy sacrifice?

2. How can we become continually transformed into Christ's image rather than being conformed to the world? How does a "renewed mind" relate to this process?

3. How, then, can we prove what God's will really is?

Footnotes

1. F.B. Meyer, *Abraham* (New York: Fleming H. Revell, 1945), p. 33.
2. Meyer, *Abraham*.

ABRAHAM'S FIRST TEST

And so, dear brothers, I plead with you to give your bodies to God. Let them be a living sacrifice, holy—the kind he can accept. When you think of what he has done for you, is this too much to ask? Don't copy the behavior and customs of this world, but be a new and different person with a fresh newness in all you do and think. Then you will learn from your own experience how his ways will really satisfy you.

Romans 12:1,2, TLB

Abraham arrived in Canaan. He had obeyed God. He had left behind a secure environment in order to follow the will of God. Once Abraham was actually in the land, God confirmed His promise; this time with more specific information.

Previously, God had promised Abraham He would *show him* the land (Gen. 12:1). Now when Abraham arrived in Canaan, God said: "To your descendants I will *give this land*" (12:7, italics added). Abraham responded with worship and praise. He built an altar to the one true God.

But Abraham's new adventure with God was just beginning. Initial obedience was merely a starting point. What lay ahead for Abraham in terms of spiritual growth? He would soon find out.

ABRAHAM'S FIRST MAJOR TEST
(Gen. 12:10)

In Holy Writ, God wasted little time in recording for us the next major event in Abraham's life. The transition appears abrupt, concise and to the point—"Now there was a famine in the land" (12:10).

This was Abraham's first test after arriving in the land. Imagine what must have gone through his mind—"I came all the way out here for *this!* I thought this was to be a land of blessings!"

This famine constituted a new experience for Abraham. As far as we know, he had never faced a famine before, not in Ur nor in Haran, which were both prosperous and productive cities. Imagine the complaining he faced from even those closest to him—"Abraham, I told you you were out of your mind to come way out here! So you obeyed your God! For what reason? So He could bring us all out here in the wilderness to destroy us?"

What irony! After his huge caravan had made it all the way across the burning desert, Abraham now faced the danger of being totally wiped out—man and beast— in the midst of the land that God had promised would provide him with blessings. Yet he could see only the prospect of losing everything he had—including his life.

Many of us tend to act quickly under pressure, especially when our human needs are not being met; and doubly so, when we're under pressure from others. Abraham faced both.

Whatever transpired, Abraham took quick action: "So Abram went down to Egypt to sojourn there, for the famine was severe in the land" (12:10).

34

A man-centered decision

Abraham acted, but he failed to consult the One who had led him to Canaan. He headed for Egypt—a land noted for its fertility and abundance.

Going to Egypt, of course, was not necessarily wrong. It was a logical step, geographically and economically. In fact, on other occasions Egypt became a place of survival and refuge for God's children. It was also in Egypt where Joseph, many years later, was used by God to provide food for his brothers and aging father when they too faced a famine in Canaan (Gen. 46:3,4). And most significantly, Egypt became a place of refuge for Jesus Christ when Herod attempted to snuff out His life (Matt. 2:13).

No, going to Egypt was not the problem. Rather, the central issue involved Abraham's taking matters into his own hands and going to Egypt *without consulting God*, the One who brought him into the land in the first place. It was a man-centered decision.

Some creative alternatives

If Abraham had looked to God for specific instructions, it is possible that God would have sent him on to Egypt anyway—but with a specific strategy on how to face the problems which he encountered when he got there. But it is also possible that God had other plans for Abraham.

Think of the creative alternatives! When God wants to meet man's needs miraculously, there is no limit to what He can do. How about providing water out of the rocks? What about manna from heaven or quail from the sea? (See Exod. 16; Num. 11:31.) How about barrels of meal that never run dry? (See 1 Kings 17.)

If God had chosen to work in this way, it would not have been the last time. For in future years, He would do things like this many times for the children of Israel as they left Egypt and journeyed through the wilderness. And had Abraham allowed God to perform these miracles, think of the testimony to the pagan Canaanites, who no doubt were laughing up their sleeves at this strange wanderer who claimed to have access to the one and only true God.

It appears that Abraham did not give God the opportunity to display His mighty power. Rather, he acted on his own, choosing what he believed was the only alternative. He "went down to Egypt."

ABRAHAM'S UNWISE STRATEGY

Abraham had barely arrived in Egypt before he began anticipating problems. Because Sarah was a beautiful and desirable woman, even at 65, Abraham feared that her presence could be dangerous for him. Abraham's fears were not without reason. History records that Egyptian men were very impressed with Semitic women. Furthermore, it was rather standard procedure in those days for men to secure women as their wives by murdering their husbands and previous possessors. Robbery and theft were not limited to gold and silver.

If Paul's account in Romans 1 describes the world of Abraham's day, mankind in general had totally deteriorated. So already knowing something of the sinful and degenerate behavior that existed around him, Abraham proposed a plan to Sarah.

Abraham's plan

"See now," he said to Sarah, "I know that you are a beautiful woman; and it will come about when the Egyptians see you, that they will say, 'This is his wife!' and they will kill me, but they will let you live. Please say that you are my sister so that it may go well with me because of you, and that I may live on account of you" (Gen. 12:11–13).

Abraham's rationalization

Abraham had a rather unique rationalization for his behavior. Sarah was indeed his sister (Gen. 11:29; 20: 12)—that is, his half-sister. She was the daughter of his father, but not the daughter of his mother. So the fact is, his planned statement to the Egyptians was but a half truth, for Sarah was also his wife (Gen. 20:12).

When Abraham arrived in Egypt his suspicions became a reality. Pharaoh, who evidently had his spies constantly on the lookout for beautiful women, quickly spotted Sarah's presence in Egypt. Natural beauty, plus her attractive foreign features, made her an easy target for money-hungry men who were working hard for brownie points with the king of Egypt. Furthermore, history records that Egyptian women were noted for their rather unattractive features, and for the fact that they "faded early," to quote some Old Testament scholars.[1]

Pharaoh wasted little time. "And Pharaoh's officials saw her and praised her to Pharaoh; and the woman was taken into Pharaoh's house" (12:15); that is, she was made a part of his harem.

It is difficult for some of us who live in the twentieth century to grasp Abraham's total reasoning. Somehow, his strong desire to save his own life, which was his basic motive, caused him to be willing to give up his own wife. But on the other hand, when we identify with Abraham's spiritual immaturity as a beginner in his walk of faith, plus the cultural pressures he faced, it is not too difficult to understand his actions. This is particularly true when we look at twentieth-century man who is often characterized by acts of deception, deceit, adultery, desertion and even murder.

Nevertheless, Abraham's actions were not right. Had he consulted God, he may have been the first man God used to convey a powerful message to the people of

Egypt—that God exists and desires to reach out to all men. Rather than falling on them in judgment, which God eventually had to do, He might have been able to extend His grace through Abraham.

If Abraham had allowed God to prepare the way for him in Egypt, his strategy would have been God-centered rather than man-centered. However, Abraham was operating under his own steam and acted from selfish motives.

God stepped in to solve the problem.

GOD'S PATIENCE AND FAITHFULNESS
(Gen. 12:17—13:4)

God's continued patience and faithfulness in the lives of His children is often amazing. This is particularly true when God selects someone to achieve a special purpose. And no purpose was more special than the one God chose Abraham to help Him achieve—the salvation of mankind.

In spite of Abraham's failures, God brought judgment upon Pharaoh for his sins (12:17). He caused Pharaoh to return Sarah to Abraham. God even allowed Abraham to keep the servants and animals which Pharaoh had given him for Sarah. In fact, Abraham was actually escorted out of Egypt, back to Canaan where he belonged. Ironically, God used pagan people to get Abraham back on the right track.

Abraham seems to have learned his lesson well. When he returned "to the place of the altar" which he had built previously, he once again "called on the name of the Lord" (13:4). This, of course, he should have done in the first place.

But remember! This man was just a beginner in his walk with God. Like so many of us, he made mistakes. But he learned from his mistakes. Do you learn from your mistakes?

KNOWING GOD'S WILL TODAY

Abraham didn't do as well as he might have in ascertaining God's will when he was presented with a major decision. How would you have responded if you had been Abraham? How can you know God's will today and avoid Abraham's mistakes? There are at least three significant lessons you can learn from this study of Abraham and his decision to go down to Egypt.

Learn from Abraham's experiences

First, *there will be frequent tests in our Christian lives.* This is really the only way we'll grow. We tend to stand still when we do not face struggles and problems. Expect them. Some of these tests God brings directly into our lives because He wants to teach us and to prepare us for a greater work for Him.

Other tests come because of the natural circumstances of life, because of the sin principle at work in this world. We must expect difficulties—physically, mentally and spiritually. We are not yet glorified.

Other problems come when we are out of God's will, and He graciously and lovingly, but often painfully to us, brings us back to "Canaan."

But here we must be careful, for God, because of His faithfulness, will at times continue to pour out blessings on us in spite of our disobedience. Our tendency is to rationalize and to continue to dabble in the world; to continue to violate His will as it is revealed in His Word. Oftentimes, the results of this kind of behavior are not immediate, but ultimate—such as having our children grow up and follow our own self-centered behavior, becoming just like us.

Second, *we, too, like Abraham, will always be tempted to go to extremes in solving our problems.* Sometimes we will even revert to strategies we used before we became Christians.

God honors good thinking and human responsibility. But we can easily get into trouble because of the ego satisfaction we enjoy when we work out problems all by ourselves. On the other hand, because we often tend to be insecure and afraid of making incorrect decisions, we may withdraw and fail to fulfill our human responsibility. It is difficult, but necessary, to maintain a balance between these two extremes.

Third, *God's faithfulness and patience continue no matter what our decisions.* This is true because He has called us to be His children; He has given us eternal life; He has promised never to leave us nor forsake us.

The danger, of course, is to interpret God's faithfulness and blessings as a confirmation that He is not displeased with our behavior:

"I'm making even more money than before."

Or, "I really feel good and secure about this decision. I'm really enjoying this relationship."

Or, "If God were really displeased, He would certainly stop using me in the lives of others."

How deceptive emotions or circumstances can be! We must never take advantage of God's love and grace.

Follow the divine order

There is a divine order in determining God's will that we must always follow; an order which Abraham forgot.

First, *consult the Word of God* to find out what He says. No doubt Abraham could have gotten word from God by direct revelation. So can we, through the Word He has already revealed. We must consult the Scriptures carefully for the directives and principles that will guide us in doing His will. When making a decision, we must always ask: Is there anything in God's Word that would teach us that this is a right or wrong decision?

Note! Be careful that you don't use the Bible as a magic book—for example, letting it fall open to a certain

40

place, allowing your eyes to fall on a certain verse, and then taking that verse out of context and using it to make a decision. That is a violation of the sound-mind principle we find in Scripture (2 Tim. 1:7).

God wants us to examine the Scriptures in order to discover His will (Acts 17:11). And the psalmist says that a wise man delights in the law of the Lord and "in His law he meditates day and night" (Ps. 1:2). It is primarily the Word of God that directs us in our lives today.

Second, *consult the body of Christ*, especially those who know the Scriptures well and who are demonstrating Christian maturity. This, of course, gives us a unique advantage over Abraham, for he had no one else to turn to but God.

There is plenty of evidence in the New Testament to demonstrate this principle. We are to be "teaching and admonishing one another" (Col. 3:16), and to "stimulate one another to love and good deeds" (Heb. 10:24). We are to "encourage one another" (Heb. 3:13), and to "pray for one another" (Jas. 5:16). In other words, the whole concept of the functioning body helps us determine the will of God.

Third, *consider the circumstances* surrounding the decision. Does it make good sense? Is it logical? Is there an overall pattern? What ultimate advantages will there be for my family? And, of course most important, how will this affect our spiritual life and maturity?

Fourth, and least important, *consider your emotions and feelings.* Consider how you feel about the decision. Imagine for a moment what would have happened if Jesus Christ had based His decision to go to the cross purely on His emotions. He probably would not have gone through with it!

The inward pain Jesus felt in the garden of Gethsemane was so great that His perspiration fell to the ground as drops of blood. He prayed that the cup of suffering and death that He had to drink would be removed. But, said He, "not My will, but Thine be done" (Luke 22:42).

Emotion can be a very deceptive element in decision making. And yet we tend to put it at the top of the list.

Any decision that involves the unknown, and most do, creates negative emotions. For years, psychologists have recognized in the decision-making process "approach-avoidance" conflicts and ambivalent feelings. It is a part of being human. Like the proverbial headache, both Christians and non-Christians also experience these negative emotions.

Interestingly, these feelings are predictable. When we are making a significant decision, it almost always involves both positive and negative emotions. And the closer we come to making the decision, the stronger the negative emotions will become. But the farther away from the decision we are, the stronger the positive emotions—which in turn makes the decision easier to think about.

Take marriage as an example. I've seen this problem particularly in older single people. The farther they are away from a decision to marry, the more comfortable they appear about the prospect. But the closer they get to saying "I do," the stronger the negative emotions may become.

When "at a distance," they are able to see all of the positive advantages of being married—love, security, a home, children, etc. But the closer they come to the decision the more sensitive they become to the negative emotions surrounding the decision—greater responsibility, loss of certain freedoms, the possibility of failure, etc.

Unfortunately, many Christians equate these emotional dynamics with the Holy Spirit. When they have negative feelings, they believe that the Holy Spirit is saying no. They feel He has taken away their "peace of mind."

When they have positive feelings, they feel the Holy Spirit is saying yes, giving them "peace of heart." The main problem with this theology is that it classifies the Holy Spirit as being ambivalent and unstable. God does not waver when it comes to His will—but we do!

The same emotional dynamics surround most every decision we make—vocational choices, where to go to school, where to invest money, how to spend money, where to live, etc. Thus we must beware of relying on our emotions. They will deceive us. In fact, many decisions have to be made in spite of negative emotions because we *know* it is the right thing to do.

There are several verses of Scripture that summarize most of what I've said so far. Two are from the Old Testament and two are from the New Testament:

"Trust in the Lord with all your heart, and do not lean on your own understanding. In all your ways acknowledge Him, and He will make your paths straight" (Prov. 3:5,6).

"I urge you therefore, brethren, by the mercies of God, to present your bodies a living and holy sacrifice, acceptable to God, which is your spiritual service of worship. And do not be conformed to this world, but be tranformed by the renewing of your mind, that you may prove what the will of God is, that which is good and acceptable and perfect" (Rom. 12:1,2).

LIFE RESPONSE

What decision are you wrestling with today? Have you presented your body, your mind, your total being to God? Have you followed through on Romans 12:1,2? Are you walking in the light of Proverbs 3:5,6?

If your answer is no to these questions, now is the time to pray this prayer, and really mean it:

"Father, I present my body to you as a living sacrifice. I know I belong to you. I'm bought with a price—the price of Jesus Christ's shed blood on the cross. I want to obey your Word. I know that I have failed you and will continue to make mistakes, but I want to be continually, and more and more, transformed into your image, reflecting Jesus Christ in my total life-style. I want to renew my mind daily as I learn more of your Word.

"And this day I give myself to you, determining in an even greater way to prove and test your perfect will for my life. I want to trust you with all my heart; I want to acknowledge you in everything; I want to use the mind you gave me, but not to rely on it and make man-centered decisions; so I claim your promise that if I meet these conditions you will always direct my paths. Amen."

FAMILY OR GROUP PROJECT

Share with your children (or with others in your group) the ways in which you have determined God's will as you've made important decisions. Encourage questions from other members of the group regarding decisions that they may be struggling with regarding knowing God's will. Close in prayer, asking God to help you to always practice the truth of Romans 12:1,2 and Proverbs 3:5,6.

Footnote

1. C.F. Kiel and F. Delitzsch, *The Pentateuch* (Grand Rapids: Wm. B. Eerdmans Publishing Co.), p. 197.

4

A SKELETON IN ABRAHAM'S CLOSET

Don't be misled; remember that you can't ignore God and get away with it: a man will always reap just the kind of crop he sows! If he sows to please his own wrong desires, he will be planting seeds of evil and he will surely reap a harvest of spiritual decay and death; but if he plants the good things of the Spirit, he will reap the everlasting life which the Holy Spirit gives him.

Galatians 6:7,8, TLB

We've all heard about the "skeleton in the closet"—a decision, an event, an act, a memory from the past that may suddenly appear to haunt us in the present. Somehow, we have camouflaged it so well that we hardly recognize it any more. But when circumstances are just right, the closet door swings open and there it hangs in all of its ugliness.

Believe it or not, Abraham had a "skeleton in the closet." And his "skeleton" was very well camouflaged, too—so much so that we often overlook it as we read his story. But it was there just the same—and clearly visible. I'm speaking of Abraham's decision regarding his nephew Lot. When certain events transpired in Abraham's life—when circumstances were just right—his closet door swung open and the skeleton called Lot was revealed for all to see, reflecting just exactly what Lot always had been and still was as a person.

You see, when God called Abraham to leave Ur of the Chaldees He made it crystal clear that His perfect will for this Mesopotamian shepherd was to leave not only his country and his own household, but also all his relatives (Gen. 12:1). We've seen already that a failure to make a complete break with his father caused Abraham at least a 15-year delay in leaving his country. And now we will see the results of his failure to separate completely from one of his relatives, his nephew Lot.

Why would God be so specific in His instructions? Why did God want Abraham to make such a complete break with those closest to him? Wasn't Abraham eventually to be a blessing to all nations? Why not begin with his father and his brother's son?

The reason appears to be related to God's awareness of future events. God is omniscient! He knows the hearts of men, now and forever.

God knew that both Terah and Lot would deter Abraham from doing His will. God was aware of their worldly hearts, their selfish motives, and He knew what their future attitudes and actions would be. God preferred to spare Abraham the problems that He foresaw. He preferred that Abraham had obeyed Him completely when He first spoke to him, so He could carry out His divine and eternal promises to Abraham.

But, as we've already seen, God is patient and long-suffering—even when behavior reflects selfish desires and insecurities. He also knew that there were certain

46

lessons Abraham had to learn the hard way. So He allowed him to journey with his father. He also allowed Abraham to have Lot accompany him all the way to Canaan.

Then the trouble came. The trouble was no surprise to God, but probably very much so to Abraham. Lot's true character surfaced. What he was and always had been down deep became a dynamic reality and revealed itself in a most insensitive and ungrateful way.

Let's look at these events in proper perspective.

LOT ACCUMULATES WEALTH (Gen. 13:5)

God was not out to "get Lot," to eventually condemn him and to prove a point. Though He knew this man's heart, His desire was toward Lot—and still is toward every man—that he might be saved from sin and self. He demonstrated His grace toward Lot and blessed him just as He blessed Abraham: "Now Lot, who went with Abram, also had flocks and herds and tents" (13:5). It appears that Lot may have actually cashed in on Abraham's Egyptian bonanza. It is a strong probability that Abraham shared with Lot the gifts of sheep, oxen, donkeys and servants that he received from Pharaoh.

If this is true, Abraham's motives for sharing his wealth may not have been entirely unselfish. Put yourself in his place. Abraham fell into enormous wealth through a man-centered strategy that left God out of the picture. He knew down deep that when he gave up his wife to a licentious and evil king he was operating from a carnal desire to save his own skin. Consequently, he felt guilty—just as you and I would. And sharing his "ill-gotten gain" may have been an attempt to alleviate some guilt.

But overall, Abraham was a sensitive and unselfish person. Generally, he was a man of character in spite of his weaknesses.

WEALTH CAUSES CONTENTION (Gen. 13:6,7)

Both Abraham and Lot were rich men. In fact, Scripture records that "Abram was *very rich* in livestock, in silver and in gold" (13:2, italics added). And as we've seen, "Lot ... also had flocks and herds and tents" (13:5). In fact, even though there was plenty of vacant land (13:9), their "possessions were so great that they were not able to remain together." Canaan "could not sustain them while dwelling together" (13:6). The result was serious strife between Abraham's and Lot's herdsmen (13:7).

Wealth can be both a curse and a blessing in a man's life. Few there are who can handle it with sufficient wisdom to keep unhappiness, jealousy and feuding away from the door. And sometimes even all the wisdom in the world won't keep it from happening.

Try as you may, even an unselfish and gracious spirit won't keep jealousy and self-centered behavior from raising its ugly head. I personally believe that the Bible teaches that Christians whom God blesses financially should invest their wealth wisely in God's work, "laying up treasures in heaven"; not storing it up for their families and other "assorted relatives" to fight over at some future date, nor allowing the government to take most of it and waste it. Nor should we spend a lifetime investing gigantic sums in pagan lawyers to help us "legally circumvent" the IRS so they won't get most of it either.

Don't misunderstand. We must be wise and responsible, providing adequately for our family's future. The Bible says that "if anyone does not provide for his own, and especially for those of his household, he has denied the faith, and is worse than an unbeliever" (1 Tim. 5:8). But some Americans—even some Christians—have a strange view of what kind of provision it will take to live comfortably and securely in this world.

And what a poor testimony this often becomes to the

non-Christian world! Abraham's concern for the pagan world was, I believe, his major consideration in the feud developing between his and Lot's herdsmen. And this is why it is recorded that "the Canaanite and the Perizzite were dwelling then in the land" (Gen. 13:7).

The quarreling wasn't caused by crowded conditions, for later Abraham reminded Lot that there was plenty of space. So why fight? (13:9). Why be a bad testimony to these pagan onlookers who were seeking every opportunity to put down Abraham's faith in the One True God.

Abraham's wealth got him into trouble rather early in his walk with God. Though his attitude was right, Abraham had no way of controlling the attitudes of those who worked for him, nor was he able to cope satisfactorily with Lot's self-centered behavior. So their herdsmen fought and feuded over who used what pastures and what waterholes and, no doubt, where they would erect their tents.

ABRAHAM OFFERS SOLUTION (Gen. 13:8,9)

In many respects, Abraham's approach to this problem is unequaled in human history: "let there be no strife between you and me, nor between my herdsmen and your herdsmen, for we are brothers" (13:8).

Abraham's attitude was magnanimous. "Is not the whole land before you? Please separate from me: if to the left, then I will go to the right; or if to the right, then I will go to the left" (13:9).

What an unselfish spirit! God had blessed Lot because of his uncle Abraham. And yet Abraham, this growing and maturing man of God, was willing to put Lot on an equal footing with him; to offer Lot a choice that could allow him to end up with a better deal than Abraham himself had.

Don't misunderstand! Abraham was not naive. He

knew what lay eastward toward Jordan—a virtual "garden of the Lord" (13:10). He knew he might come out with the worst of the land. But his love for Lot, his desire for unity and peace, and his concern about his personal witness in a pagan community became more important than his own material welfare.

LOT CHOOSES THE BEST (Gen. 13:10–12)

The moment Lot had a choice, and the moment Abraham gave him an opportunity to make a decision on his own, his true character surfaced! He "lifted up his eyes and saw all the valley of the Jordan, that it was well watered everywhere . . . like the garden of the Lord, like the land of Egypt as you go to Zoar" (13:10).

Oftentimes a carnal Christian's problems begin with his "eyes." It's what he sees and experiences that precipitates wrong decisions. How true this was of Lot! His Egyptian experience that resulted in greater possessions also stimulated a taste for more and better.

Lot was vulnerable and susceptible. His choice, which eventually had a positive effect on Abraham's life, had a negative effect on Lot and his family. As a result of his choice Lot became even more deeply rooted in the things of the world. The "valley of the Jordan" had in it the city of Sodom—one of the most degenerate cities in the world at that time. If Lot was aware of this fact, it didn't deter his selfish and carnal decision.

And so he "chose for himself all the valley of the Jordan; and Lot journeyed eastward. Thus they separated from each other. Abram settled in the land of Canaan, while Lot settled in the cities of the valley, and moved his tents as far as Sodom" (13:11,12).

GOD REASSURES ABRAHAM (Gen. 13:14–18)

God's response to Abraham should be reassuring to any Christian who is struggling to make a decision based on unselfish motives. God's response was the third specific revelation that Abraham received in his pilgrimage with his new Friend.

"And the Lord said to Abram, after Lot had separated from him, 'Now lift up your eyes and look from the place where you are, northward and southward and eastward and westward; for all the land which you see, I will give it to you and to your descendants forever. And I will make your descendants as the dust of the earth; so that if anyone can number the dust of the earth, then your descendants can also be numbered. Arise, walk about the land through its length and breadth; for I will give it to you' " (13:14–17).

The first revelation Abraham received was when God called him to leave Ur. God said: "Go forth from your country . . . to the land which I will show you" (12:1). Then when Abraham had obeyed God fully by leaving the city of Haran, crossing the desert and eventually coming into the land of Canaan, God again appeared and became more specific in His promise: "To your descendants I will give this land" (12:7). In other words, "This that you see is the land I promised you when you still could not see it."

Now again, when Abraham makes a final surrender and separates from his nephew Lot, giving up the best part of the promised land unselfishly and in faith, God becomes more specific in His revelation and tells Abraham that his unselfishness will be rewarded a thousandfold. "You haven't given up anything, Abraham, in view of what you and your descendants will eventually receive."

With every step of obedience came greater light and reassurance. This is the way God frequently works with men. The more we do His will, the more we understand regarding His master plan for our lives. Though our journey may be marked by famine and even painful encounters with those closest to us, God has our interests at heart. He wants His best for us.

Obviously, Abraham at this time did not clearly understand the meaning of all that God had said. The eternal aspects of this promise were no doubt rather elusive. But whatever his understanding at this juncture in his life, there came a time when he understood more fully. The writer of Hebrews says: "By faith he [Abraham] lived as an alien in the land of promise, as in a foreign land, dwelling in tents with Isaac and Jacob, fellow-heirs of the same promise; for he was looking for the city which has foundations, whose architect and builder is God" (Heb. 11:9,10).

TWENTIETH-CENTURY SKELETONS

All of us have made decisions and participated in certain activities in our past lives that tend to haunt us in the present. When circumstances are just right—or wrong—memories and feelings of these wrong decisions and activities can be triggered within us.

How should a Christian handle his twentieth-century skeletons? In the same way that Abraham dealt with his. He faced it realistically, objectively and obeyed God.

Fundamentally and basically, we must realize that a person who is truly a Christian need not worry about skeletons. The Bible says: "Therefore if any man is in Christ, he is a new creature; the old things passed away; behold, new things have come" (2 Cor. 5:17).

From God's perspective, He does not remember our skeletons. And we need not remember them, either. Nor should we as Christians remember the skeletons in the lives of others.

As Paul said, "From now on we recognize no man according to the flesh." Even though we are still living in this body and subject to failure, and will be until Christ comes again, we should view ourselves and other

52

Christians as God views us. We are made perfect in Christ. And this should be our message to others and a constant reminder to ourselves, that "God reconciled us to Himself through Christ" (2 Cor. 5:14–21).

Many people misinterpret this passage—especially 2 Corinthians 5:17. Some believers think that to be in Christ means that everything—body, soul, and spirit—becomes new the moment we receive Christ. Not so! Pure logic based on observation confirms this conclusion.

We do not automatically receive a new body when we receive Jesus Christ personally. Nor do we automatically receive a new soul—that is, a new intellect, a new set of emotions. Nor do we automatically receive a new will.

But we do receive a *new position* in Christ—and as far as God is concerned, when we receive Christ personally we are already seated with Him in heaven (Eph. 2:6). From His perspective we are already glorified (Rom. 8:30). In other words, God does not look at our past lives nor our present weaknesses and judge us. We are truly forgiven.

Not only do we receive a new position in Christ, we also receive a *new nature*—a capacity to become more and more like Christ in our behavior. Unfortunately, this is not automatic. We do not immediately become like Christ. Many of us continue to reap what we have sown after we become Christians.

Paul tells us that if we have sown to the flesh, we will reap corruption (Gal. 6:7,8). There is no way to completely undo what we have already done; sin has affected our bodies and our psychological nature. But God still sees us as "perfect in Christ."

However, we should not be satisfied with our present state. Paul wrote that we are not to be conformed to this world, but be transformed by the *renewing of our minds*

53

(Rom. 12:2). We are to become more and more like the Saviour.

But let's be realistic and practical. How do we handle these skeletons from the past?

First, as we've already emphasized, we must *have a correct theological view of conversion.* The Bible seems to classify men as having three major parts—body, soul and spirit (1 Thess. 5:23; Heb. 4:12). Functionally, this seems to correlate with the physical, psychological, and spiritual dimensions of man's personality (see fig. 1). To be a non-Christian means we are spiritually dead—that is, we have not been reconciled to God. We do not have a *new position* in Christ nor do we have a *new nature* with the capacity to renew our minds in Christ.

However, both Christians and non-Christians may function quite well in their physical and psychological nature. When Adam sinned, causing the whole world to be affected, God did not take away from man his capacity to become a balanced personality physically and psychologically. There are many non-Christians who are quite mature in these areas of their lives, in some instances, causing them to feel that they don't even need Jesus Christ. They are quite comfortable without Him.

When we become a Christian, then, we do not receive a new body (a new physical nature), nor do we receive a new soul (a new intellect, a new set of emotions, a new will). Rather, we bring to conversion what we are in these areas of our lives—our strengths and our weaknesses.

We do, however, receive a *new position* in Christ (we are made alive to God), and we receive a *new nature* or capacity that will enable us to grow and develop spiritually, affecting our total being.

Keep in mind, however, that if we have sown to the flesh we have already reaped corruption in our bodies and our souls. Change may come rather slowly, and in

54

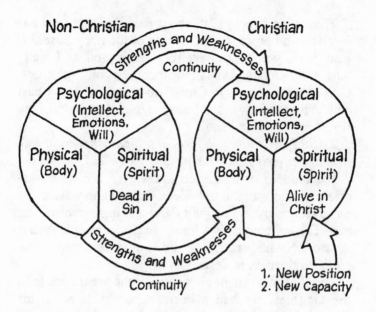

Figure 1

some instances, we must realize that we will have to live with certain problems in our lives.

Also, some Christians may find that emotional and physical problems may get worse before they get better. Because new Christians have a new conscience code and a new standard of behavior, their stress and anxiety level may rise. But they must always remember that while they are in a transition from the old to the new life, God still sees them perfect in Christ. Their sins have been washed away. There is no need to allow these "skeletons" to haunt them.

A *second* practical step in dealing with skeletons in the past is to *develop a strategy for handling them.* The following questions will help you analyze the situation:

1. *Do I feel guilty about things I shouldn't feel guilty about?*

55

That is, do I feel guilty about past sins that God has forgiven and buried in the depths of the deepest sea? If I do, I really may not have forgiven myself, or I really may not understand the biblical concept of forgiveness. God sees me perfect in Christ, no matter what my past and no matter how much I have reaped the results of my sin in my body and soul.

2. *Do I feel guilty as a form of self-punishment, trying to make myself righteous in God's sight?*

We tend to do this, you know. We are so works-oriented that we tend to believe that we can wash away our own sins by feeling guilty and making ourselves feel bad. This, of course, is a form of self-deception. And it is also a Satanic trick, not allowing us to accept complete forgiveness in Jesus Christ.

Think for a moment about Paul—the great apostle to the Gentiles. He had a horrendous "skeleton in his closet." As a non-Christian, he had severely persecuted Christians and had actively participated in murdering Stephen, a great New Testament Christian. But when he became a believer himself, he forgot what lay behind and reached forward to that which lay ahead. "I press on," he wrote to the Philippians, "toward the goal for the prize of the upward call of God in Christ Jesus" (Phil. 3:14).

If you are a Christian, you, too, can forget the past, and you can help other Christians forget the past. This does not mean you will not remember the event, the decision, the act! But it need not haunt you and make you feel guilty or bring you into bondage. You are forgiven. Any time Paul thought about his past, he recognized and rejoiced in God's marvelous grace—that he, the chief of sinners, had discovered salvation in the Lord Jesus Christ.

But what about the carnal Christian who deliberately continues to sin against God—who continues to develop

56

"skeletons" in his Christian life? In our next chapter we'll look at Lot, an Old Testament example of a carnal Christian. The results were devastating and his end was tragic! So stay tuned!

If "skeletons" from the past constantly haunt you, there is a strategy for dealing with them.

LIFE RESPONSE

Do you know what it means to really and experientially have your sins forgiven? Do you have a correct theological view of conversion and Christian growth? If you cannot answer yes to these questions, face your personal need and do something about it today. The following steps will assist you:

1. *Make sure you have truly confessed your sins to God and accepted His forgiveness.*

2. *If necessary, ask forgiveness of others you have sinned against.*

3. *If necessary, make restitution.* Note that steps 2 and 3 are not necessary before you receive forgiveness from God. They may not be necessary at all. But sometimes they are necessary to set you free from yourself.

4. *Renew your mind* (your psychological nature) *by exposing yourself to God's truth in the Scriptures.*

5. *If you continue to be plagued by guilt, seek help from someone else.*

You may find it very helpful to share your problem with a mature Christian who will listen to you, understand you, pray for you and help set you free from your "skeleton"—from your bondage. James writes: "Confess your sins to one another, and pray for one another, so that you may be healed" (Jas. 5:16).

Note: Here is a warning to young people! Remember that we *do* reap what we sow. Don't deliberately live your life in such a way that you will actually produce "skeletons." Psychological problems and physical

57

deterioration are not automatically changed through conversion.

Fortunate, indeed, is the person who becomes a Christian, bringing to his conversion experience a healthy mind and body, free from nagging guilt and other problems. But remember also that not all psychological and physical problems are because of specific sins. Because of our human weaknesses and the sin principle that is at work in the world, we have sufficient natural tendency toward deterioration without aggravating the situation through a direct violation of God's moral laws.

FAMILY OR GROUP PROJECT

Review this chapter and discuss ways you can specifically apply these concepts to your individual life experiences. Read Psalm 1 and discuss how this scriptural passage correlates with the message of this chapter.

5

A DISASTROUS DECISION

But remember this—the wrong desires that come into your life aren't anything new and different. Many others have faced exactly the same problems before you. And no temptation is irresistible. You can trust God to keep the temptation from becoming so strong that you can't stand up against it, for he has promised this and will do what he says. He will show you how to escape temptation's power so that you can bear up patiently against it.
1 Corinthians 10:13, TLB

A study of Abraham's life remains incomplete without a careful look at Lot's selfish and ungrateful decision to leave his uncle and move toward Sodom. And that initial decision precipitated a life of carnality and deterioration that led to a sad and pathetic end for Lot. His life demonstrates dramatically the fallacy of attempting to deliberately live outside of God's revealed will.

Regarding Lot's decision, let's explore three basic questions. First, what was the *basis* of that decision? Second, what was the *process* involved? And third, what were the *results?*

THE BASIS OF LOT'S DECISION (Gen. 13:10)

Why did Lot make such an unfortunate decision to move his tents toward Sodom?

He was influenced by what he saw

This is very clear from the text of Scripture. He "lifted up his eyes and saw all the valley of the Jordan, that it was well watered everywhere . . . like the garden of the Lord, like the land of Egypt as you go to Zoar" (13:10). Lot's eyes became the windows to his soul which triggered selfish desires that caused him to forget or ignore everything his uncle Abraham had ever done for him.

Lot's response was cumulative—as it always is. He had already had a taste of the "good" life. His uncle Abraham had already shared much of his wealth with him. Like most people, he wanted more. Furthermore, he had experienced the lush pasturelands of Egypt, and the Jordan valley offered the same luxury.

He was influenced by what he heard

We can easily conjecture that he had probably heard some rather intriguing and spicy stories about the city of Sodom, a place known for its immorality. Our twentieth-century "live sex shows" and "X-rated movies" would be mild compared with what was taking place in Sodom. It was "sin city" in the Old Testament world, one of the most wicked places anywhere on earth.

He excused and rationalized his decision

Perhaps he thought: "Uncle Abe has more than I have anyway, this will just balance everything out."

Or, "Old Uncle Abe is kind of naive—he doesn't really care. After all, he gave me my choice."

Or, regarding Sodom, Lot might have said to himself, "That wicked city really needs a strong witness for the Lord. After all, who's going to tell them about God?"

Or perhaps he felt his family needed a little "broader exposure" to the world! After all, his uncle Abraham was getting pretty religious—building altars all over the place and calling on the name of the Lord.

Whatever his rationalizations or excuses, Lot's decision was based on his own selfish desires. He did not consult God about it. In fact, he left God completely out of the picture. He did not think very long—if at all—about how this decision would affect his uncle. He did not consider the negative effect the city of Sodom might have upon his children and himself. His choice was based entirely on what the apostle John calls "the lust of the flesh and the lust of the eyes and the boastful pride of life" (1 John 2:16). What he saw and heard attracted him, and without regard for anyone else, he made up his mind.

THE PROCESS OF LOT'S DECISION (Gen. 13:10–12)

The steps that led to Lot's self-centered decision and actions are very clear in this story. And they are usually inherent in every decision man makes, good or bad.

He saw

"Lot lifted up his eyes and saw." How many times have you ever done something wrong or foolish because you first *saw* something you wanted? Most of man's greatest failures can be traced back to the "lust of the eyes." In fact, this is the way sin first entered the human race: "When the woman saw that the tree was good for food, and that it was a delight to the eyes, and that the tree was desirable to make one wise, she took from its fruit and ate; and she gave also to her husband with her, and he ate" (Gen. 3:6).

Many years later, one of the most talked about sins of Israel also began with the eyes. One evening, when King David had a lot of time on his hands, he "arose from his bed and walked around on the roof of the king's house, and from the roof he saw a woman bathing; and the woman was very beautiful in appearance" (2 Sam. 11:2).

The rest of the story is well known. He sent for Bathsheba and committed adultery. Later, caught in a trap he had set for himself, he committed murder to try to escape the results of his first sin.

One sin led to another. Consequently, he paid the price for his sins the rest of his life. Though God forgave him, David never escaped from the results. Another result of David's sin was the destructive impact it had on his children. Because of their father's poor example, David's children committed many sins in Israel.

Yes, most sins begin with what we *see.* Lot was no exception.

He chose

Lot "chose for himself all the valley of the Jordan." Very few sins are committed without first *choosing* to do so.

Daniel stands head and shoulders above many Old Testament saints in demonstrating purity in the midst of temptation. When his eyes were really attracted to the royal foods in the king's palace, even as a young man he "made up his mind that he would not defile himself with the king's choice food or with the wine which he drank" (Dan. 1:8). And he didn't!

Every act of sin, or every decision *not* to sin, involves making up our minds. Lot *chose* to indulge himself in the "lusts of the flesh."

He acted

Lot *separated* himself from Abraham. He "moved his tents as far as Sodom." He "settled in the cities of the valley" (Gen. 13:11,12).

First, man *looks,* second he makes a *choice,* and finally he *acts* on his choice. He goes after what he has seen.

Again, when man faces temptation he either indulges in the sin or he flees and moves in the opposite direction. Joseph is another example of a great Old Testament saint who acted positively rather than negatively. For many days as a servant in Potiphar's house he was tempted by Potiphar's wife. But he had made up his mind that to yield would be wrong—a sin against God and his master. And one day he was tempted far beyond what he'd seen and heard. "She caught him by his garments, saying, 'lie with me!'" (Gen. 39:12).

How easy it would have been for Joseph to rationalize his behavior, as David did, but he didn't. "He left his garment in her hand and fled . . . outside" (Gen. 39:12).

THE RESULTS OF LOT'S DECISION (Gen. 19:1–38)

Lot's self-centered and carnal choice eventually led him into very serious trouble, as this kind of decision always does. God inspired Moses to record at length all that followed Lot's decision, because He wants us to be aware of the results of self-centered decisions. Though these details are rather graphic—the Bible is an honest book—they serve as a serious warning to any person who is tempted to play with fire. You cannot escape without getting burned!

Lot was subject to great harassment and demands

He who makes close friends with sinful and wicked people sooner or later faces disappointment. Real friendship is based on mutual respect and concern, not selfishness. Genesis 19:4–7,9, tells about Lot's "friends": "Before they [the angels] lay down, the men of the city, the men of Sodom, surrounded the house, both young and old, all the people from every quarter; and they called to Lot and said to him, 'Where are the men who came to you tonight? Bring them out to us that we may have relations with them.' But Lot went out to them at the doorway, and shut the door behind him, and said, 'Please, my brothers, do not act wickedly! ... But they said, 'Stand aside.' Furthermore, they said, 'This one came in as an alien, and already he is acting like a judge; now we will treat you worse than them.' So they pressed hard against Lot and came near to break the door."

Lot lost all sense of moral values

This man, seems to have lost his ability to discern right from wrong. He became totally inconsistent and confused. His behavior became bizarre. He tried to protect two men (total strangers) from sexual abuse and, of all things, offered his own daughters instead: "Now behold, I have two daughters who have not had relations with man; please let me bring them out to you, and do to them whatever you like" (19:8).

It's difficult to explain Lot's behavior, except to point out that people who fail to obey God in one area of their life often deteriorate in other areas as well. Eventually they lose all sensitivity to sin, particularly in the area of morals. Moral deterioration is the worst kind of deterioration. Lot was like an airplane pilot in a fog without instruments. He lost all sense of direction.

Lot lost his influence over those closest to him

Even the men who were going to marry Lot's daughters lost respect for him. When he tried to warn them of coming judgment, they ignored him. They did not take him seriously. They thought he was jesting (Gen. 19: 14). They did not believe in God in the first place, so why should they believe in a coming judgment?

The people of Sodom went right on eating, drinking, buying, selling, planting and building—and continued their immoral actions (Luke 17:28).

64

Lot lost his will to do what was right

This is a very serious step downward in spiritual and moral deterioration. Even in the context of a direct revelation from God—knowing what God's will was—Lot hesitated to leave his sinful environment. He seemingly succumbed to the influence of his pagan sons-in-law. Evidently their refusal to take his warnings seriously demoralized Lot so significantly that he, too, found it difficult to believe that judgment was really coming.

If it weren't for God's grace and love for Lot—in spite of his sinful behavior—he would have been destroyed with everyone else in Sodom. We read that "the men [who had been sent by God] seized his hand and the hand of his wife and the hands of his daughters, for the compassion of the Lord was upon him; and they brought him out, and put him outside the city" (Gen. 19:16).

At this point remember *why* God was showing compassion on Lot—only because of Abraham, the man Lot had treated so disgracefully. It was Abraham who had pleaded with God to preserve Lot and his family from total destruction (Gen. 18:22–33).

Lot took advantage of God's grace

Even in the midst of God's compassion and overt efforts to save him, Lot did not want to obey God completely. God had told him to escape to the mountains in order to be safe, but he imposed on God's grace and asked for an alternate solution. Again God's compassion was upon Lot and He granted him his request to go to a small town nearby called Zoar (Gen. 19:19–23).

Lot lost his most prized possession—his wife

Perhaps the most bitter result of Lot's decision to move to Sodom was the influence on his wife. No doubt, she felt so secure with the life-style of this sinful city that she could not bear to leave it. Though she was forcibly

65

led out of the city, she wanted to go back. She fell behind, looking back toward the city with great disappointment.

When God rained brimstone and fire from heaven, she evidently was too close to the city and literally turned into a charred statue. She didn't make it out of the valley in time because she was dragging behind—looking back. She became a pillar of salt.

Lot committed sin with his own daughters

Here again we see the influence of Sodom. Lot's daughters had also lost all sense of moral rightness. They were more concerned with their own posterity than with obedience to God and respect for their father (see Gen. 19:30–38).

And so ends the tragic story! Lot is never mentioned again in the Abrahamic story or in the rest of the Old Testament.

At this point some will ask whether or not Lot was truly an Old Testament saint. Did he really have a personal relationship with God?

The apostle Peter answered these questions very succinctly: "If He [God] condemned the cities of Sodom and Gomorrah to destruction by reducing them to ashes, having made them an example to those who would live ungodly thereafter; and if He rescued *righteous* Lot, oppressed by the sensual conduct of unprincipled men (for by what he saw and heard that *righteous* man, while living among them, felt his *righteous* soul tormented day after day with their lawless deeds), then the Lord knows how to rescue the godly from temptation, and to keep the unrighteous under punishment for the day of judgment, and especially those who indulge the flesh in its corrupt desires and despise authority" (2 Pet. 2:6–10, italics added).

Three times Peter uses the word "righteous" to describe Lot, indicating that Lot must have been a true believer. But he was carnal. He made a self-centered decision that led him into deep sin. He eventually paid a terrible price for his disobedience. In most instances, Christians who live in sin do not face immediate judgment from God, but rather bring judgment on themselves through the natural consequences of sin.

A NEW TESTAMENT PERSPECTIVE

Most of us who live carnal and undisciplined Christian lives follow the same process Lot followed when we are making decisions. We are first tempted by what we *see*, then we make a *choice*, and finally, we *act* upon that choice. And like Lot, we often rationalize our behavior, coming up with some of the most unique and preposterous excuses for doing what we do.

The New Testament Christians faced the same problems we do. Paul had to speak to that issue—especially when he wrote to the Corinthians. True, they were Christians, but most of them were carnal and fleshly Christians. They were living for Satan and themselves, not Jesus Christ. Consequently, Paul wrote: "And I, brethren, could not speak to you as to spiritual men, but as to men of flesh, as to babes in Christ. I gave you milk to drink, not solid food; for you were not yet able to receive it. Indeed, even now you are not yet able, for you are still fleshly" (1 Cor. 3:1–3).

Later, Paul said "if any man builds upon the foundation [Christ] with gold, silver, precious stones, wood, hay, straw, each man's work will become evident; for the day will show it, because it is to be revealed with fire; and the fire itself will test the quality of each man's work. If any man's work which he has built upon it remains, he shall receive a reward. If any man's work is burned up, he shall suffer loss; but he himself shall be saved, yet so as through fire" (1 Cor. 3:12–15).

Lot is an Old Testament example of a carnal Christian. And in his carnality he destroyed himself. His refusal to do the will of God led him to a bitter end. Though eventually he was saved, his whole life was characterized by a miserable existence. Paul wrote: "Do not be deceived, God is not mocked; for whatever a man sows, this he will also reap" (Gal. 6:7).

The story of Lot is an extreme case. Most of us cannot identify directly with the depth to which he fell. But we can identify with the process. Every day of our lives the world holds out its attractions to us.

There are so many things to see, to look at, to think about—things that dull our sensitivity to God and His Word. We don't even have to go looking! These things come to us. How easy it is to make a choice, and before we know it we are acting on that choice.

For you, it may be an inordinate desire for material things that dulls your sensitivity to God. For another, it may be sexual temptation—through what you see and think about. For others it may be something else. You know your own heart and you know what it is! There is only one solution! We must look the other way, make up our minds that we will not sin against our Lord, and then act in the will of God.

Psalm 1 provides a beautiful pattern for overcoming temptation. Note the process spelled out in verse 1. Once we act on a bad choice, we are *seated* in the midst of sinful people. This is exactly what happened to Lot. When we encounter him in Genesis 19, he is "sitting in the gate of Sodom" (19:1).

By contrast, Abraham acted in the direction spelled out in verse 2 of Psalm 1, and the results in his life are graphically illustrated in verse 3. And though Lot appears to have been a true believer—though a carnal one—his life on this earth is graphically described in verse 4. Read this psalm and see the pattern:

1. How blessed is the man who does not walk in the counsel of the wicked, nor stand in the path of sinners, nor sit in the seat of scoffers!
2. But his delight is in the law of the Lord, and in His law he meditates day and night.
3. And he will be like a tree firmly planted by streams of water, which yields its fruit in its season, and its leaf does not wither; and in whatever he does, he prospers.
4. The wicked are not so, but they are like chaff which the wind drives away.
5. Therefore the wicked will not stand in the judgment, nor sinners in the assembly of the righteous.
6. For the Lord knows the way of the righteous, but the way of the wicked will perish.

LIFE RESPONSE

Make a choice today that will lead you in the direction of spirituality—not carnality. Be specific. What is your greatest temptation? Your greatest weakness? Attack it with your whole heart and soul. Program your mind for victory in Jesus Christ—not for failure! Remember, 1 Corinthians 10:13: "No temptation has overtaken you but such as is common to man; and God is faithful, who will not allow you to be tempted beyond what you are able; but with the temptation will provide a way of escape also, that you may be able to endure it."

FAMILY OR GROUP PROJECT

Study carefully and memorize 1 Corinthians 10:13. Consult several versions. Discuss some of the temptations that face twentieth-century Christians. What are some of the ways God has provided avenues of escape? Using the truths in this chapter, what must we do to avoid sinning against God?

6

ABRAHAM'S BOUT WITH FEAR

For the Holy Spirit, God's gift, does not want you to be afraid of people, but to be wise and strong, and to love them and enjoy being with them. If you will stir up this inner power, you will never be afraid to tell others about our Lord.

2 Timothy 1:7,8, TLB

Have you ever traveled along in life feeling rather comfortable with your life-style? Everything appeared to be going your way. You were decisive, you felt good, your level of self-confidence amazed even you; and—most meaningful to you—you felt good about God. You seemed close to Him, you trusted Him, and you sensed that you were doing His will.

Abraham experienced the same spiritual and emotional dynamics. He appeared comfortable with his life-style; he was making bold and forthright decisions. He put God first in his life. Then—like many Christians today, particularly when they are making good progress —Abraham faced an emotional and spiritual crisis. His mind and heart suddenly filled with fear. He became afraid! What had been dynamic, decisive and courageous behavior suddenly turned into feeble, ambivalent and fearful reactions.

THE CONTEXT OF ABRAHAM'S FEAR (Gen. 14:1–23)

What happened to change Abraham's attitude? In order to understand how the twentieth-century pilgrim can effectively cope with similar circumstances, let's look at the *context* and *cause* of Abraham's sudden fear, and also the later *change* in his perspective.

Abraham's magnanimous attitude toward Lot

We've already noted Abraham's unselfish and generous actions toward his nephew. When strife arose among their herdsmen, Abraham offered Lot an unprecedented choice. He could select the section of land that best suited him and Abraham would take what was left. Lot, of course, chose the best, leaving his uncle Abraham with the more barren and unproductive environment. Abraham's reaction was indeed a remarkable demonstration of self-denial, self-control and self-sacrifice. In New Testament language, he "turned the other cheek" toward an ungrateful, self-indulgent and egotistical relative who was interested only in feathering his own nest.

Abraham's defense of Lot

When Lot, this self-seeking man, separated from his uncle, he soon got himself involved with the people of Sodom. "He was living in Sodom" (14:12), when he and his whole family were taken captive by four warring kings who swooped down and attacked several cities in the vicinity of Sodom and Gomorrah. These kings "took all the goods of Sodom and Gomorrah and all their food supply, and departed. And they also took Lot, Abra-

71

ham's nephew, and his possessions and departed" (14: 11,12).

When Abraham heard about Lot's capture "he led out his trained men, born in his house, three hundred and eighteen, and went in pursuit as far as Dan. And he divided forces against them by night, he and his servants, and defeated them, and pursued them as far as Hobah, which is north of Damascus. And he brought back all the goods, and also brought back his relative Lot with his possessions, and also the women, and the people" (14: 14–16).

This was a bold and courageous maneuver by Abraham. He laid his own life and the lives of the men who served him on the line for a selfish and conceited nephew. Here was a gracious and kindhearted man who held no grudges, no bitterness, and no animosity toward a brother who had taken advantage of him. Abraham indeed represents an Old Testament example of living for Jesus Christ, of doing God's will in spite of difficult circumstances, and of Christian obedience.

Abraham's refusal to identify with the world

When Abraham returned from doing battle with the four warring kings, he was met by the king of Sodom, who obviously was grateful for Abraham's act of love. For Abraham recaptured not only Lot, his family and his goods, but also a number of other Sodomites and their possessions. In his gratitude "the king of Sodom said to Abram, 'Give the people to me and take the goods for yourself' " (14:21).

Abraham's response must have been shocking to the king of Sodom: "I have sworn to the Lord God Most High, possessor of heaven and earth, that I will not take a thread or sandal thong or anything that is yours, lest you should say, 'I have made Abram rich' " (14:22,23).

At that moment Abraham refused to identify with the

immorality and degenerate paganism in Sodom. He turned his back on what the world would classify as a golden opportunity, an opportunity to cash in on a real bonanza.

What consistency! Abraham had been left with the more unproductive section of Canaan. Lot's selfish actions may have caused Abraham to face some real hard times, a factor that could have made Abraham's refusal of the spoils of battle a difficult decision. He could have really used those "goods." But he still refused! He let the king of Sodom know, in no uncertain terms, that he worshiped "the Lord God Most High" who was capable of meeting his needs. After all, Abraham's God was the "possessor of heaven and earth." And since God owns "the cattle on a thousand hills" (Ps. 50:10) Abraham at this moment was able to trust God for his future needs.

THE CAUSE OF ABRAHAM'S FEAR (Gen. 15:1–3)

What could have caused Abraham to move from such boldness to a state where it was necessary for God to reassure him, "Do not fear, Abram," (Gen. 15:1). Well, Abraham was human! And he did have some pretty good reasons to feel fear.

Have *you* ever made a series of brave and, from a human point of view, what may appear in retrospect to be rather naive and perhaps even reckless decisions? This, I believe, was Abraham's predicament! Think with me for a moment what the consequences of Abraham's decision might have been.

The threat of retaliation

Abraham, with his small band of "trained men" had taken on four kings with their armies of highly trained warriors. It is logical to assume that they could retaliate at any time and wipe out this whole family and all his servants, or take all of them into slavery. It would have been rational for Abraham in a moment of reflection to ask himself, *"What have I done?"* And furthermore, "For what purpose?" The grave answer would have to be, "I've risked my neck and the lives of my whole household for a selfish and ungrateful nephew."

The threat of poverty

Not only had this Old Testament saint risked annihilation or slavery, he had just turned down an offer of material possessions that rightfully belonged to him anyway, and that he no doubt could have used. Lot had chosen the fertile valley of the Jordan and left Abraham in danger of poverty. His mighty herds and flocks would have quickly eaten every living herb that was struggling to grow in this rather desolate land, just recovering from a very severe famine.

A predicament that made God's promises hard to believe

God had promised Abraham a *land*, a *seed* and a *blessing*. At this point Abraham had no security of any of these promises, so he must have been doubting everything God had said.

The most pressing lack of these three promises, however, was the fact that Abraham had no "seed," no natural son. How could he develop into a great nation? At one time, perhaps, he had thought that Lot might have been a means for God to fulfill His promise. But that hope was quickly dissipated when Lot turned away from him and from God.

So Abraham faced an unusual problem. He turned to God, his only source of help, and said: "O Lord God, what wilt Thou give me, since I am childless, and the heir of my house is Eliezer of Damascus? . . . Since Thou hast given no offspring to me, one born in my house is my heir" (15:2,3).

74

THE CHANGE IN ABRAHAM'S PERSPECTIVE
(Gen. 15:1–6)

With Abraham's bold attack on the four armies, he had just put his whole life and existence on the line! Earlier, he had taken God at His word, stepped out on faith and moved into a strange land. He had unselfishly given up the choicest parts of his promised land; he had rescued his ungrateful nephew; and he had refused to identify with a worldly system.

As a result of his boldness and unselfishness, Abraham now faced a possibility of retaliation from the defeated kings, poverty from his own actions and a future without a progeny through whom God could fulfill His promise. Given the same circumstances, how would you react? Abraham must have gone into a state of shock. He must have felt a great deal of anxiety and fear.

But God did not forsake Abraham. The Lord again communicated with him. One by one, God spoke directly to every one of the events that had brought Abraham into this emotional and spiritual crisis.

"Do not fear, Abram, I am a shield to you"
(Gen. 15:1)

Abraham's initial concern was a fear of retaliation. But God promised him He would be his "shield," against foreign warriors. Here we see an Old Testament example of the New Testament admonition to "put on the full armor of God, that you may be able to stand firm against the schemes of the devil" (Eph. 6:11).

"Do not fear, Abram ... your reward shall
be very great" (Gen. 15:1)

Abraham's second concern involved his potential poverty. He had just turned down a bountiful reward from the king of Sodom, saying, "I will take nothing" (Gen. 14:24), so that he could be God's total man. And once again we see God's reassuring words, a restatement of His promise to Abraham that he would be abundantly rewarded for his faithfulness.

"Do not fear, Abram ... you *will* have descendants" (Gen. 15:6)

Humanly speaking, Abraham had cause to be worried and afraid, and God understood. Accordingly, God once again gave Abraham reassurance, revealing His promise to His friend in even greater detail than previously. In the darkness of the night, perhaps when Abraham was tossing and turning on his bed with fear and anxiety, God "took him outside and said, 'Now look toward the heavens, and count the stars, if you are able to count them.' And He said to him, 'So shall your descendants be' " (15:5).

This dramatic experience with God once again gave Abraham security, quieted his nerves and dissipated his fears. We read: "Then he believed in the Lord; and He reckoned it to him as righteousness" (15:6).

God honored Abraham's faith. In fact, it was the means of his personal salvation (see Rom. 4:1–3). "In hope against hope he believed, in order that he might become a father of many nations, according to that which had been spoken, 'So shall your descendants be.' And without becoming weak in faith he contemplated his own body, now as good as dead since he was about a hundred years old, and the deadness of Sarah's womb; yet, with respect to the promise of God, he did not waver in unbelief, but grew strong in faith, giving glory to God, and being fully assured that what He had promised, He was able also to perform" (Rom. 4:18–21).

No man has ever been saved by works. It has always been by faith. Abraham looked forward to the cross; we look backward to the cross. And we are all made righteous in Jesus Christ. "Therefore," said Paul, after illustrating salvation with Abraham's experience, "having been justified by faith, we [too] have peace with God through our Lord Jesus Christ" (Rom. 5:1).

FEARFUL CHRISTIANS

Few believers in the twentieth century will ever experience the specific *context* and *causes* of Abraham's fear. But we will consistently face the same emotional and spiritual dynamics. Though circumstances vary throughout history, man's feelings are basically constant. In his basic needs, Abraham was no different than you or I. He was a human being.

Let's review and illustrate what happened. (See fig. 2.) Abraham had a basic *need*—a need to be secure. His *goal* was to do the will of God. His *behavior* was to step out by faith and obey God. He separated from Lot at a loss to himself; he defended Lot even after Lot turned against him; he refused to identify with an immoral society.

But in the process Abraham hit a wall of frustration. He faced the threat of poverty; he faced a strong possibility of retaliation from his enemies; and he faced the fact that he still had no natural heirs to receive the covenant of God. The result was *fear* and *anxiety.*

Abraham's reaction to all this was exemplary. Evidently he cried out to God. And, as we've seen, God reassured Abraham that He would help him surmount his wall of frustration.

How does all this apply to the twentieth-century Christian? We, too, face walls of frustration. Our physical, psychological and spiritual needs are many. We are constantly striving to reach goals that will meet our needs. But within our environment are many obstacles to reaching our goals. There are conflicts that create constant anxiety. They may be a financial problem, a personal inadequacy or a conflict of interests.

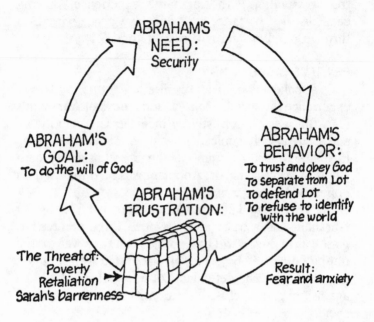

Figure 2

The question all of us must face is: How do we handle frustration? Fear is a natural reaction. Some Christians —because of fear—retreat, become immobile and unproductive. They try to run away from the problem. Anger is another natural reaction, though it is a more immature response. Those who become angry and aggressive try to *break* the wall down, caring little about others' feelings and needs.

LIFE RESPONSE

What wall of frustration are you facing today? Are you responding in a mature way?

Following is a list of questions that will serve as a checklist to help you analyze your maturity level:

1. *Am I facing reality?* Do I recognize that the wall of frustration is actually there and that it is real?

2. *Have I gained God's perspective on the problem?* Do I know what God says in His Word about this problem? Have I sought His solution?

3. *Am I trusting God in the midst of this problem?* Do I really believe that He cares and that He meant it when He said He would never leave me or forsake me?

4. *Have I decided on a sensible and logical solution?* For example, does God want me to circumvent the wall? Does He want me to dismantle it and remove it? Does he want me to climb over it? Does he want me to wait until He supernaturally removes it? Does He want me to wait a while? Or does He want me to change my goal?

All of this, of course, takes wisdom. But remember that God says: "If any of you lacks wisdom, let him ask of God, who gives to all men generously and without reproach, and it will be given to him" (Jas. 1:5).

Remember, too, that the Bible says: "And we know that God causes all things to work together for good to those who love God, to those who are called according to His purpose" (Rom. 8:28).

Whenever you face a wall of frustration, be sure to stop and ask yourself, "What can God teach me in this difficult experience? How can He make me a more mature Christian?" You'll be amazed at the inner strength God gives you as you *trust Him* and *believe* in His promises in the midst of these frustrating situations.

FAMILY OR GROUP PROJECT

As a family, make a list of obstacles, problems, and conflicts that create frustration in your life. Then, using the questions in the checklist, decide on a possible solution to these problems.

7

A RIGHT MOTIVE— A WRONG METHOD

Work hard so God can say to you, "Well done." Be a good workman, one who does not need to be ashamed when God examines your work. Know what his Word says and means.

2 Timothy 2:15, TLB

Is it possible to have a right reason for doing something and to go about it in the wrong way? Most of us don't have to think too hard or long about this question. The answer is a decided yes, and Abraham proved it! The next major event in his life demonstrates that his motive was right—but his method was wrong!

ABRAHAM'S PREDICAMENT (Gen. 15:4—16:1)
From a human perspective, Abraham still faced a serious problem. And in one respect his dramatic encounter with God, recorded in Genesis 15, added to his dilemma. God had spoken to Abraham and confirmed His covenant to make him a father of a great nation. In fact, God became very specific. Abraham's heir would come

from his "own body!" (15:4). His "descendants" would be as the stars! (15:5). And though they would be in captivity in a foreign land for many years, his descendants would eventually return to the land that God would give them—the land of Canaan (15:13,14).

After God reconfirmed His covenant with Abraham, Abraham asked for a visible sign, "O Lord God, how may I know?" (15:8). God answered by use of a common ceremony, one that was familiar to Abraham. In those days two parties would enter into a covenant by selecting certain animals and birds, cutting them in half —except the birds (15:10)—and laying them out in two lines. Then both parties of the covenant would pass between the lines to confirm the contract. Either party who then violated the contract would be subject to the same fate as the animals—death.

So God said to Abraham, "Bring Me a three year old heifer, and a three year old female goat, and a three year old ram, and a turtledove, and a young pigeon" (15:9). So Abraham gathered the animals, cut them in two and laid them out according to the custom. Then God performed the miracle. After dark, "there appeared a smoking oven and a flaming torch which passed between these pieces" (15:17). In this way God confirmed His covenant with Abraham.

Even though God promised to give "to your descendants . . . this land" (15:18) Abraham still faced a perplexing problem. Sarah was barren! In fact, she had *never* borne children (16:1). Furthermore, she was already beyond the normal age when women conceive. How could he and Sarah produce a son? Humanly speaking, of course, they could not!

Abraham was seriously troubled about this predicament. True, he had believed God when He had promised him a son. In fact, he *still* believed God! But as time passed he became more and more bewildered. It had been more than 10 years since he had first entered Canaan. How could God's promise be fulfilled?

SARAH'S PROPOSAL (Gen. 16:1,2)
While Abraham was pondering his plight, Sarah—bless her heart—came up with what she thought was a good suggestion. There are two aspects of Sarah's proposal that seem very significant.

The content of Sarah's proposal
Sarah offered her maid, Hagar, as a substitute mother. Hagar was an Egyptian. She was probably one of the "female servants" Abraham had obtained as a gift from Pharaoh (Gen. 12:16). Abraham was again about to encounter problems as a result of his man-centered decision to go to Egypt during the famine. His involvement with Hagar would be another consequence of his failure to consult God.

The reasoning behind Sarah's proposal
Sarah used "religious reasoning" to support her proposal. "Now behold," she argued, "the Lord has prevented me from bearing children" (16:2). What better rationale could she use than to involve God in their predicament? After all, He had promised Abraham a son who would come from "his own body." And, as far as we know, God had said nothing specifically about Sarah's part in this event. So since Sarah had never borne children, and was now past the age of conception, could it be that God wanted to use another woman to achieve His purpose?

Somehow it never seemed to enter Sarah's mind, or Abraham's, to consult the God who had supernaturally led them out of Ur, the One who had preserved them from annihilation as they had crossed the burning desert; the One who had rescued them from their blunder in Egypt and returned Sarah to Abraham; the One who had just appeared to Abraham in a vision and, with a miraculous sign, confirmed the promises He had spoken directly to Abraham on several occasions. Somehow it never occurred to Abraham and Sarah that the One who had denied children to Sarah for so long could just as easily give them to her now.

Furthermore, though it seems rather strange to us today from our historical vantage point, Abraham again did not consult God about Sarah's proposal. Couldn't the "Lord God Most High," the "possessor of heaven and earth," the One who had promised to be Abraham's "shield" and "reward"—couldn't He cause Sarah to bear a son? At this moment where was Abraham's recent perspective on God? (Gen. 14:22,23).

Before we judge this Old Testament saint too severely, let's look more specifically at Abraham's predicament and some of the thoughts that may have passed through his mind.

ABRAHAM'S PARTICIPATION (Gen. 16:2–4)

From our New Testament perspective on Christian morality, what Abraham did may shock us. Especially since he was a man who was so intent on doing the will of God. But we must realize that Abraham's motive was right! He had no evil intentions.

Abraham was actually attempting to do the will of God! He was bent on helping God achieve His purpose. But even though his motive was right, Abraham's reasoning was faulty. As a result, he made three big mistakes.

Abraham's first mistake

Abraham wrongfully assumed that Sarah's arguments were valid. True, she was barren, and God hadn't specifically stated that Sarah would be the woman to bear his son. But for Abraham to act on this premise was to limit God, especially in view of the Lord's forthright promises to Abraham.

Abraham's second mistake

Abraham assumed that Sarah's offer was based on truly unselfish motives. True, what she did certainly appeared to be very unselfish. And in many respects it was. She, too, was concerned about God's will. Also she was concerned about Abraham's emotional state—his sorrow and anxiety resulting from his predicament. But the events that transpired later indicate that Sarah's proposal was also prompted by some very selfish motives.

The psychological phenomenon of mixed motives is not really an uncommon one. It is probably impossible for sinful mankind, even in a converted state, to act out of totally pure motives. Underneath are often selfish motives that even those who are the closest to us cannot detect. In some respects, this is probably more of a blessing than a curse. But in Abraham's case, Sarah's mixed motives became more of a curse than a blessing. He again made a wrong decision in not consulting with God about this matter.

Abraham's third mistake

Abraham allowed thought patterns and practices he had learned from his pagan culture to influence his thinking. What Sarah had proposed was a very common practice in those days. Certain tablets containing marriage contracts discovered by archaeologists "specify that a barren wife must provide a woman for her husband for the purpose of procreation."[1] In fact, "many of the unusual actions of [both] Abraham and Jacob with regard to marriage and children can now be understood as being part of the prevailing social culture and laws that Hurrians and Babylonians alike followed for centuries in the Middle East."[2]

You see, both Abraham and Sarah were still in transition. They were still shedding the aspects of their pagan upbringing that were in contradiction to the will of God. This was no doubt especially true of Sarah. She, more than Abraham, was still highly influenced by her pagan life-style. And in this instance, though Abraham was committed to one woman, he found himself vulnerable to Sarah's proposal.

This explanation, of course, in no way condones Abraham's actions. It does help to understand them. But even though his motive was right, his method was wrong. Though he was sincere in his efforts, he made serious mistakes. Once again he stepped out of the will of God.

THE RESULTS OF ABRAHAM'S MISTAKES
(Gen. 16:4–6)

Abraham had been deceived, both by his wife and by himself. And, as with most of us when we make serious mistakes, the results of Abraham's wrong decision, like chickens, quickly came home to roost. Three things happened immediately.

Hagar became proud and arrogant

The moment Hagar conceived, she became proud and arrogant. She despised Sarah (16:4). When Abraham replaced his wife with an Egyptian servant, he violated God's moral law as well as His psychological laws.

We read in Proverbs: "Under three things the earth quakes, and under four, it cannot bear up: Under a slave when he becomes a king, and a fool when he is satisfied with food, under an unloved women when she gets a husband, and *a maidservant when she supplants her mistress*" (Prov. 30:21–23, italics added).

Hagar's behavior was predictable. If Abraham had stopped to think about this situation, he may have even come to this conclusion on his own. But more important, if he had consulted God, he would have gotten a clear perspective on why this would be a serious error.

Sarah became bitter

Not only did Sarah become bitter and vent her wrath on Hagar, but she also turned on Abraham. In her insecurity, she lashed out at the one who had simply followed her suggestion. "And Sarah said to Abram, 'May the wrong done me be upon you. I gave my maid into your arms; but when she saw that she had conceived, I was despised in her sight. May the Lord judge between you and me'" (16:5).

F.B. Meyer succinctly captures the irony of Sarah's actions: "How true this is to human nature! We take one false step, unsanctioned by God; and when we begin to discover our mistake, we give way to outbursts of wounded pride. But instead of chiding ourselves, we turn upon others, whom we may have instigated to take the wrong course, and we bitterly reproach them for wrongs in which they, at most, were only instruments, whilst we are the final cause."[3]

Abraham passed the buck

The third result of Abraham's mistake surfaced when Abraham's original predicament became worse. Not only did he not solve the problem of a legitimate heir but he created an almost unbearable tension in his household. And rather than face the responsibility as the head of his household, *he dumped the problem back on Sarah.*

"Behold," he said, "your maid is in your power; do to her what is good in your sight" (16:6). Sarah, in her state of insecurity and anger toward Hagar, treated her harshly. Consequently, the maidservant "fled from her presence" (16:6).

THE INTERVENTION OF GOD (Gen. 16:7–15)

Again God intervened, as He had done when Abraham made his mistake in Egypt.

God had mercy on Hagar

An "angel of the Lord found her by a spring of water in the wilderness" (16:7) and told her to return to her home and to submit to Sarah's authority. And the Lord also promised her she would have many descendants. Hagar did return, and she bore Abraham a son who was named Ishmael (16:15).

God came to Abraham's rescue

Despite Abraham's wrong decision and its unfortunate consequences, God continued to carry out His unconditional promises to Abraham. But Ishmael's birth began a new chapter in world history that has not yet ended. From Hagar's son has come the great Arab nations who have in recent years plagued the children of Israel, the promised seed of Abraham. They are still suffering from Abraham's mistakes—mistakes born out of a right motive on Abraham's part, but from a wrong method.

DETERMINING RIGHT METHODS TODAY

As with all Old Testament events, we can learn some tremendous lessons from Abraham's mistakes. But first, let's review Abraham's situation with a twentieth-century technique (see fig. 3).

Abraham faced another wall of frustration. There was nothing wrong with his motive or his goal. He wanted to do the will of God, and his specific goal was to produce a godly seed, as God told him he would. But his wall of frustration was a barren wife. The result of this frustration was a general state of anxiety. His method for solving the problem was to follow Sarah's suggestion and obtain a son by means of Hagar, her Egyptian maid. Unfortunately, this was a wrong strategy, an inappropriate method, a serious mistake, and it led to increased tension and accentuated Abraham's anxiety.

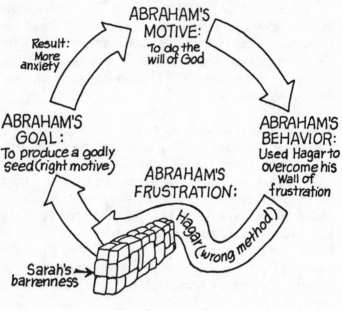

Figure 3

What can we learn from Abraham's mistake that will help us select right methods and develop appropriate strategies to overcome barriers and walls of frustration that we face in living the Christian life? We must remember that God actually had not given Abraham specific directions in this matter, only general guidelines. This is true to a great extent in our lives today. In many situations God has merely given us general principles to guide us in making intelligent decisions.

How then can we know God's will? What dangers should we avoid in selecting methods to carry out God's will in matters where the Word of God is basically silent?

There are at least five lessons and principles we can learn from this biblical account that will help us make intelligent decisions in carrying out the will of God.

1. *We must be on guard against the human tendency to take matters into our own hands.*

The first question we usually ask when we face a wall of frustration is: "What can I do?" Not, "What does *God* want me to do?" Obviously, this was to a great extent Abraham's problem. Rather than reflecting back on previous experiences where he faced similar predicaments and trying to learn from past successes and mistakes, he got "locked in" to the existential moment—a situation which always tends to blur man's thinking. He didn't even consult God about the matter.

2. *We must be on guard against making quick decisions and snap judgments.*

This also was part of Abraham's problem. He was not sensitive to timing. He got in a hurry. True, 10 years seemed like a long time to Abraham. But a little reflective thinking would have reassured him that God was not in a hurry to work out His plan. God had told Abraham in his previous vision that he would die before the promise of the land to his descendants would be fulfilled. In fact, God told him his descendants would be in captivity for at least 400 years before they would settle in Canaan.

There are times, of course, when we must act quickly. But there are also times when we must wait to take action. Better to wait and gain a proper perspective than to rush in and make a serious mistake. Remember, too, problems that are difficult to solve create an opportunity for God to display His power and guidance. Perhaps this is why He wants us to wait.

3. *Even those closest to us—those we trust the most— can lead us astray.*

Sarah's perspective, though it appeared unselfish, was humanistic and man-centered. Furthermore, she was very emotionally involved with Abraham.

A godly wife or husband should be able to serve as a good sounding board for decision-making. But remember, even though Sarah was loyal to Abraham she was not spiritually mature. Even when a spouse *is* godly, sometimes they are so close to the problem they cannot be objective. It is advisable to consult more objective members of the body of Christ as well as those closest to us when making important decisions.

4. *We must beware of the subtle influence of our former life-style in determining the will of God.*

Culture has a way of permeating our personalities and molding our thinking. It has a way of creating an influence that lingers in our minds and influences even our Christian lives.

This was part of the problem with Abraham and Sarah. Choosing to use a woman other than Sarah to insure an heir to the promise was a part of their cultural laws. Why not use an approved practice to solve this problem and overcome their frustration?

Beware, then, of the custom-made set of colored glasses we all have as a part of our perceptive apparatus. When we become Christians we need to check our "spiritual and psychological eyesight" with the direct teachings of Scripture. And we must interpret Scripture correctly and consult with other mature members of the body of Christ.

5. *We must always select methods and strategies that are in harmony with principles and guidelines of Scripture.*

Generally, God does not spell out specific methods and strategies for solving problems. Rather, He gives us principles and guidelines for making decisions, just as He has done in this biblical account of Abraham. True, He gives us many specific directives that are clear-cut:

"Thou shalt love thy neighbor as thyself";

"Thou shalt not commit adultery";

"Thou shalt not steal";

"Thou shalt not be unequally yoked with an unbeliever"; etc. (see Lev. 19:18; Exod. 20; 2 Cor. 6:14.)

But in most situations involving twentieth-century decisions regarding vocation, marriage, education and business, God expects us to use the minds He has given us to think our way through these situations.

But we must never select methods that contradict God's nature or the way He works with man. If we do, we will make the end justify the means—and like Abraham and Sarah, we'll compound our problems. This is why, of course, we must saturate our minds with the Word of God so that we can know the will of God.

LIFE RESPONSE

Review the lessons we can learn from Abraham's experience by means of the following checklist. Note those that you tend to violate the most in your approach to decision-making. Then pray and ask God to help you apply these principles when you face your next decision in determining God's will.

☐ Taking matters into my own hands without consulting God.

☐ Making quick decisions and snap judgments without gaining a comprehensive perspective on the situation.

☐ Leaning too heavily on the judgments of those closest to me.

☐ Being unaware of how my thinking and judgments

91

can be influenced by my previous life-style and value system.

☐ Being unconcerned about making sure my methods and strategies are in harmony with God's principles.

FAMILY OR GROUP PROJECT

Apply these lessons to specific situations in your family or small group. What kind of decisions can these biblical guidelines help you make in your family life or group relationships?

Think of decisions in which you've violated these principles. What resulted?

Think of decisions in which you applied these principles. What were the results?

Footnotes

1. *Wycliffe Bible Encyclopedia* (Chicago: Moody Press, 1975), 1:741.
2. *Wycliffe Bible Encyclopedia*, 1:810.
3. F.B. Meyer, *Abraham* (Old Tappan, New Jersey: Fleming H. Revell Company, 1945), p. 98.

8

A WRONG METHOD—ANOTHER MISTAKE

If you want favor with both God and man, and a reputation for good judgment and common sense, then trust the Lord completely; don't ever trust yourself. In everything you do, put God first, and he will direct you and crown your efforts with success.

Proverbs 3:4–6, TLB

Is it possible to make a mistake and yet believe you're doing the perfect will of God? Is it possible to be totally sincere and yet do what God is displeased with? Abraham, of course, has already demonstrated this possibility. He had a pure motive when he got Hagar pregnant. He was trying to help God along. But he was wrong! He made a serious mistake. And he began to pay the consequences immediately.

For the next 13 years Abraham believed that he had been in the will of God when he fathered Ishmael. It appears that he continued to think he was in the will of God, in spite of the family problems created by Ishmael's birth. In fact, it seems that Abraham even interpreted certain circumstances as a confirmation of God's earlier promise to him when in fact these circumstances had nothing to do with God's previous revelation.

These events in Abraham's life teach us a dramatic lesson about the most subtle form of self-deception. It is possible for us to make one mistake which can lead to another, even without our knowing it. A Christian can think he's doing the will of God, that he is on the right path, when actually he took the wrong turn sometime back. And as we will see in Abraham's story, when this happens, it becomes very difficult to admit to ourselves and to others that we've made a mistake.

ABRAHAM'S INITIAL MISTAKE IN PERSPECTIVE

There is no doubt about Abraham's sincerity in attempting to do God's will. But his intense desire to help God fulfill His promise involved him in a strategy that led him into serious error.

God had promised Abraham a son, an heir. And this child would come from Abraham's own body (Gen. 15: 4). The Lord, possibly testing Abraham's faith and his reliance on Him for help, did not specifically indicate that Sarah would be the mother.

Because Sarah could not bear children, Abraham's logic—prompted by Sarah's suggestion and supported by cultural practice—led him to conclude that some other woman would be the mother of his son. So when Sarah herself suggested Hagar, the Egyptian slave, Abraham willingly participated in the plan. After all, from a human perspective, it appeared to be the only logical thing to do!

But Abraham's logic was wrong. This was not God's plan. Hagar bore Abraham a son, but he was not the promised seed. And as we've seen, the moment Ishmael was born, Abraham's family life was temporarily devastated. However, the negative effects of Abraham's mistaken logic were not temporary; they created incredible problems for him far into the future.

ABRAHAM'S INITIAL ERROR IN LOGIC LED TO ANOTHER

What happened next is one of the most dramatic and significant lessons twentieth-century Christians can learn from the Old Testament. Abraham continued to depend on his own faulty logic in evaluating future events and even concluded that what he observed coincided with God's previous revelation. This, of course, is the most subtle form of confused thinking, because it appears to be so right!

But let's look at what happened. Sarah's jealousy exploded in Abraham's face; then turned into harsh and bitter actions, driving Hagar into the wilderness. There an angel of the Lord appeared to this Egyptian maid, and instructed Hagar to return to Sarah and submit to her authority. Then the Lord revealed a significant message to Hagar, one that would sound familiar to Abraham: "I will greatly multiply your descendants so that they shall be too many to count" (Gen. 16:10).

Obviously, Hagar shared this revelation with both Abraham and Sarah when she returned. And what would be Abraham's logical conclusion? God's promise to multiply Ishmael's descendants sounded almost identical to His previous promise to Abraham. In the midst of Abraham's bout with fear, had not God said, "Now look toward the heavens, and count the stars, if you are able to count them ... So shall your descendants be" (Gen. 15:5).

God's message to Hagar regarding Ishmael seemingly led Abraham to another error in logic. Did not this message from God confirm the fact that Abraham had done the right thing in bringing Ishmael into the world by means of Hagar? *Because* Abraham was sincere, *be-*

cause his first decision seemed logical in view of God's promise, *because* a son actually was born and *because* God's revelation to Hagar regarding Ishmael's future sounded so much like His promise to Abraham, this Old Testament saint falsely concluded he indeed was in the will of God and that Ishmael was the promised heir.

ABRAHAM FACED THE SILENCE OF GOD

Abraham, of course, was wrong. Ishmael was not the promised seed. And Abraham's mistake in taking matters into his own hands set the stage for one of the most difficult lessons a child of God can learn. God let his servant wander in the wilderness of his own mistakes for 13 silent years. Abraham was 86 years old when Hagar gave birth to Ishmael, and it wasn't until he was 99 that God again appeared to him and spoke directly about His will. (See Gen. 16:16; 17:1.) Even more significant, Abraham actually believed he was still in the will of God during this period of silence.

Think of it! In spite of his family problems, Abraham struggled ahead for 13 years, thinking he was doing God's will. How painful this experience must have been. Never, since Abraham left Ur, had God been so far away and for so long a time.

But God was teaching Abraham a dramatic lesson, one He often teaches His children. When a child of God takes matters into his own hands and tries to do things all by himself, God sometimes lets him do it, and then allows him to struggle in the darkness that he himself has created.

But God's purpose is always for our own good, to teach us to trust Him with all our hearts, to lean not upon our own understanding, and to acknowledge Him in everything—and all because He wants to direct our paths into His perfect will (see Prov. 3:5,6).

This was God's desire for Abraham, and His loving

discipline was at work in this man's life. The next time He spoke to Abraham, God knew He would have a man who would listen—a man whose heart was truly prepared to become the father of many nations.

ABRAHAM'S LATER DIFFICULTY IN ACCEPTING GOD'S WILL

When God eventually broke the period of silence with a direct revelation to Abraham, He made it very clear that the heir He had spoken of over 13 years before was not Ishmael. The promised son was yet to be born!

And Sarah was to be the mother of the inheritor of the covenant (Gen. 17:16), not Hagar nor any other woman!

What a shock this must have been to Abraham! For 13 years he felt he was on the right track. Everything had appeared to be so logical, so rational.

"Then Abraham fell on his face and laughed" (Gen. 17:17). This verse has puzzled many Bible interpreters. Why would Abraham fall on his face and laugh? Why would he question God's power to give him and Sarah a son in their old age, especially in view of God's reassuring words (see Gen. 17:16)? Why would he cry out to God: "Oh, that Ishmael might live before Thee! (Gen. 17:18)?

Some have concluded that this must have been an exclamation of joy! But how could it be? This would be strange behavior indeed. The context seems to make the meaning clear. This was a nervous laugh! It was a laugh reflecting doubt and confusion!

Abraham's reactions were those of a man who had felt he was right and suddenly discovered he was wrong! He was a man who had placed his total hope in Ishmael as the promised seed. He had come to love this obstreperous child, in spite of his wild nature (see Gen. 16:12). It was only logical for him to defend himself and his son at this moment, to question God about the event and to plead for Ishmael.

But God's answer was a clear-cut "No!" "Sarah your wife shall bear you a son, and you shall call his name Isaac; and I will establish My covenant with him for an everlasting covenant for his descendants after him" (Gen. 17:19).

No wonder Abraham was shocked! The statement sounded like a contradiction. Had God not told Hagar He would bless Ishmael with many descendants? Was Ishmael not the promised seed?

You see, though Abraham's thought patterns seemed logical, they were confused. Consequently, he had difficulty accepting the fact that he had made a serious mistake. To discover he was outside of the will of God for all those years when he thought he was in the will of God, was a rather devastating experience. It was a shattering blow to Abraham's ego.

But at this point, God's grace toward Abraham and Ishmael is abundantly clear, in spite of Abraham's mistake. The Lord very graciously reassured Abraham regarding Ishmael's future—"I will bless him, and I will make him fruitful, and will multiply him exceedingly. . . . I will make him a great nation" (Gen. 17:20).

For the first time in 13 years Abraham was able to understand God's revelation to him (Gen. 15:5) as well as the one to Hagar (Gen. 16:10). It now made sense. God was talking about two sons. The first was Isaac; the second was Ishmael. The first was the true heir; the second was born according to the flesh.

The most encouraging part of this story is its ending. Abraham, true man of God that he was, took immediate steps to get back on the right track with God. He saw his error. Though he could not undo the past (he had to live with the results of that error), he immediately began to obey God's word. The Lord gave Abraham a new contract, a covenant in the flesh—circumcision—a sign of separation from all that is contrary to the will of God. Once the fog had cleared in Abraham's thinking, he immediately obeyed God with the rite of circumcision (see Gen. 17:22–27).

A TWENTIETH-CENTURY LESSON

One mistake *can* lead to another—and often without our knowing it. This was Abraham's problem. Abraham didn't seem to be aware of his first mistake; consequently he didn't recognize the second one. In a sense, he was like a pilot flying blind—not because there were no signals, but rather because he attempted to move ahead on his own, ignoring the signals. Abraham didn't consult God.

Abraham's experience is intriguing, and it is relevant to twentieth-century Christians. Even though his motive was right, his method was wrong. He actually thought he was helping God fulfill His divine purpose. By not consulting God about the matter, Abraham erred in logic! And that error led to another one. The more Abraham used his own logic and saw their conclusions, the more they appeared to conform to the will of God. Abraham was unable to discern the sometimes subtle distinctions between right and wrong. His thinking was blurred even though it appeared to be clear.

This can happen to us in the twentieth century. It can happen when we do not consult God's Word. It can happen when we ignore the advice of spiritually mature brothers and sisters in Christ. It can happen when we get our egos involved and try to take matters into our own hands. It can happen even in a moment when we sincerely desire to do God's will.

And when we make a decision without God's leading, believing we are right, we are in danger of attributing the outcome of future activities to our own "right" decision.

Like Abraham, we can even misinterpret the Word of God, using it to support our prejudices and biases.

And then, when we suddenly discover our mistake, sometimes even years later, we have difficulty admitting it, accepting it and getting back on the right track. It's traumatic and threatening to change thought patterns, to admit we've been wrong. But here we can learn a valuable lesson from Abraham. Though it was a difficult revelation for him to accept, he immediately obeyed God. He got back on the right path. True, he couldn't undo the past. That was ever with him. In fact, his mistake would rise up to haunt him for years to come. But he obeyed nevertheless. And as we'll see, God blessed him for his faithfulness and obedience.

LIFE RESPONSE

How can we avoid Abraham's mistake? Or perhaps a more specific question: What can we do to make sure we are not a victim of subtle deception?

The following criteria will assist any Christian in avoiding this problem:

1. *We must be aware of Satan's subtle strategy to deceive us.* He will do anything to lead us astray (Eph. 6:10–12). He may even appear "as an angel of light" (2 Cor. 11:14).

2. *We must recognize that our own heart is deceitful* (Jer. 17:9). We may even be sincere in wanting to do God's will, but there is always the tendency toward selfish actions.

3. *We must be aware of our tendency to think subjectively and with personal biases.* If we want something badly enough, we can interpret almost anything as being a positive sign of God's approval and blessing.

4. *We must be on guard against pride.* Once we've made a mistake, it is very difficult to admit to ourselves and to others that we have been wrong.

5. On the positive side, *we must recognize that we are in a much better position than Abraham to evaluate God's will.* We have the completed revelation of God. Though at times God may appear to be silent, in actuality He is not, for He has already revealed all we need to know to live in His perfect will. Though we may lose our focus or perspective, we always have the Source to whom we can go for sufficient direction to discover the error of our way.

6. Perhaps most important, *we must remember it is never too late to get back on the right track.* In some instances, as with Abraham, we may have to carry the burden of our previous mistake, but this is no excuse for not being able to enjoy the present and future blessings of being in God's perfect will.

FAMILY OR GROUP PROJECT

Review Abraham's story. Then discuss the six steps for avoiding Abraham's mistake. Discuss some specific ways in which Satan deceives us; specific ways in which we may deceive ourselves; how pride stands in the way of being in God's perfect will. Then pray and ask God to help each of you to avoid these pitfalls.

9

ABRAHAM'S NEW PERSPECTIVE

I, therefore, the prisoner of the Lord, entreat you to walk in a manner worthy of the calling with which you have been called.

Ephesians 4:1

God had not spoken directly to Abraham for 13 years —ever since Abraham had taken matters into his own hands to try in his own way to produce a godly seed. Abraham was already "eighty-six years old when Hagar bore Ishmael to him" (Gen. 16:16). And he "was ninety-nine years old" when "the Lord appeared" to him again (Gen. 17:1).

We have walked with Abraham this far through the pages of Scripture, and we have come to know his strengths as well as his weaknesses. It takes very little imagination for us to conclude this was a very difficult time for Abraham. During this long period of spiritual drought there was no new revelation. God was silent.

"It must have been a terrible ordeal," states F.B. Meyer, "driving him back on the promise which had been given and searching his heart to ascertain if the cause lay within himself. Such silences have always exercised the hearts of God's saints, leading them to say with the Psalmist: 'Be not silent to me: lest, if thou be silent to me, I become like them that go down into the pit' (Ps. 28:1). And yet they are to the heart what the silence of winter is to the world of nature, in preparing it for the outburst of spring."[1]

God was preparing Abraham and Sarah for their next significant step of faith. Seemingly, there are certain lessons that many of us will never learn unless we have periods of crisis and despair. Unfortunately, this is our human tendency—we could learn in other ways, but we choose not to.

Sometimes God has to lovingly hit us over the head with a two-by-four before He can get our attention. It is only then that we really learn who God is and how we can walk before Him in holiness. Thus when God once again spoke to Abraham, this was His message—"I am God Almighty; walk before Me, and be blameless" (Gen. 17:1).

WHO GOD IS!

God is called by many names, but this is the first time He revealed Himself as God Almighty, *El Shaddai*. Heretofore, the primary name by which He revealed Himself was *Elohim*, meaning the God who makes nature; who causes it to be; who preserves it. *El Shaddai*, on the other hand, refers to the God who constrains nature, the One who actually causes nature to do what is against itself.

You see, it is one thing for God to create the universe and its natural laws—to cause the sun, the moon and the stars to revolve in their orbits, to establish the laws of gravity and other predictable phenomena. But it is yet another thing for God to cause the sun to stand still and the moon to stop (Josh. 10:12,13) supernaturally.

God created nature and its laws and even though He

103

ordained that the natural laws govern the universe in an orderly and predictable manner, God is capable of reversing these laws, of working miracles within the natural order of His creation. He is the omnipotent God, the One who is not limited in power.

Abraham and Sarah had yet to discover and trust God as One who could and would work miracles that transcend nature. True, they had come to know God as a personal God, One who loves mankind and wants to communicate with us. They had experienced God as their Shield and Protector. They had seen Him superintend their lives, protecting them as they journeyed from Ur to Canaan, delivering them from the hand of Pharaoh, and protecting them from the four warring kings of Canaan.

But Abraham and Sarah were unable to interpret God's specific promise of a seed as a supernatural phenomenon. They could only view this process through human eyes. From their perspective, they had to help God out. From their point of view, God was not capable of causing Sarah to produce a child when she was barren, especially when she was already beyond the normal age when women bear children. This lack of perspective on God's power and ability led them to make a serious mistake.

But God used their error to teach them, and us, a tremendous lesson—*that He is God Almighty!* He is capable of working miracles, of actually turning nature against itself. He created natural laws; He can violate natural laws.

Significantly, when God appeared to Abraham with a new name, El Shaddai, He also gave Abraham and Sarah new names. "No longer," said God, "shall your name be called Abram [meaning, 'exalted father'], but your name shall be Abraham" [meaning, "a father of a multitude"] (Gen. 17:5). And, "as for Sarai your wife, you shall not call her name Sarai, but Sarah shall be her name [meaning 'princess']. . . . I will bless her . . . and she shall be a mother of nations" (Gen. 17:15,16).

God gave them names that in their very meanings were reminders of His promise and His power to fulfill that promise. And to do so at the very same time God appeared to Abraham as El Shaddai, is just another expression of God's grace and desire to reach out to men. His silence had not been punishment and revenge, but loving discipline and training to help Abraham walk by faith and to fulfill God's perfect will. And Abraham learned that lesson well!

Listen to the apostle Paul's reflections on what happened: "In hope against hope he believed, in order that he might become a father of many nations, according to that which had been spoken, 'So shall your descendants be.' And without becoming weak in faith he contemplated his own body, now as good as dead since he was about a hundred years old, and the deadness of Sarah's womb; yet, with respect to the promise of God, he did not waver in unbelief, but grew strong in faith, giving glory to God, and being fully assured that what He had promised, He was able also to perform" (Rom. 4:18–21).

HOW TO WALK BEFORE GOD! (Eph. 4:1—5:17)

After the Lord revealed Himself as God Almighty, He zeroed in on a second lesson He was teaching Abraham during the 13 silent years, "Walk before Me, and be blameless" (Gen. 17:1). This truth, of course, is a natural corollary to the first. A correct perspective on God (who He is and what He has done and is continually doing for us) should result in a godly life.

Abraham had failed in his walk with God. Though his motives were right he had sinned nevertheless. He had failed to consult God. He had become impatient. He had taken matters into his own hands. He had departed from

God's perfect will. Now, he was ready to listen, to eagerly do what God wanted him to do. This, of course, was a sign of a man whose heart was warm and tender toward the God he loved, even though he failed along the way.

To "walk before God" and "to be blameless" literally means to be "complete" or "perfect." This does not mean being sinless or perfect in the absolute sense. If this is what God meant, then we would become like God Himself while on earth—an utter impossibility.

We are always subject to sin and continue to fall short of God's moral perfection and standard every day of our lives. But it *is* possible to live before God in such a way that our lives are continually reflecting the life of Jesus Christ more and more. And the more we truly come to know God's love, power, and grace toward us, the more we will want to become like His Son Jesus Christ, who revealed the Father to us (see John 1:14).

The greatest New Testament commentary on these two Old Testament lessons that God taught Abraham is Paul's letter to the Ephesians. Of all the New Testament correspondence, this letter stands out as the most complete in its biblical teaching and doctrine and instruction on how to live in the light of biblical truth.

In the first three chapters of this epistle, Paul describes the mighty power and grace of God involved in His plan of redemption. In reality, this redemptive plan was the fulfillment of the very promise that God made to Abraham, that through him all nations of the earth would be blessed. That promise spoke clearly of the coming of the Lord Jesus Christ to be the Saviour of the world. Paul was so caught up with the excitement and thrill of presenting God's great redemptive plan that he ended the first section of the letter with a glorious doxology, "Now to Him who is able to do exceeding abundantly beyond all that we ask or think, according to the power that works within us, to Him be the glory in the church and in Christ Jesus to all generations for ever and ever. Amen" (Eph. 3:20,21).

But following this presentation of who God is and what He has done, is doing and will do for His children, Paul next exhorts believers regarding *how they are to walk before God.* Five times he told the Ephesians to walk before God so as to be mature and complete.

"Walk in a manner worthy of the calling with which you have been called" (Eph. 4:1)

This is the same lesson God was teaching Abraham many years before. God had graciously and sovereignly called him out of a pagan environment, out of his lostness, and had led him to a new country. He had protected him, provided for him, and promised to never forsake him, nor his children yet to come. In fact, His promises were eternal. And now, said God, following Abraham's sin with Hagar, "I am God Almighty; walk before Me, and be blameless" (Gen. 17:1). In other words, "Walk worthy, Abraham, of your great calling."

"Walk no longer just as the Gentiles ... walk" (Eph. 4:17)

Again, this is the same lesson Abraham was learning. He had reverted to a pagan life-style and practice when he tried to produce the promised seed through Hagar. No longer was he to live this way.

The Gentiles Paul described were no different than those who lived in Abraham's day. They, too, were "darkened in their understanding, excluded from the life of God." They, too, had hardened their hearts and had "given themselves over to sensuality, for the practice of every kind of impurity with greediness" (Eph. 4:17–19). So when God told Abraham to "walk before Me, and be blameless," He was saying to Abraham what

107

Paul said to New Testament Christians: "Walk no longer just as the Gentiles ... walk."

"Walk in love" (Eph. 5:2)

Abraham had already learned some significant lessons about love. His attitudes and behavior toward his nephew Lot were no doubt unparalleled in the pagan world. But as with every child of God, he still had more to learn, especially in his love toward God. Little did he realize at this point how God would test his love. That lesson still lay ahead!

"Walk as children of light" (Eph. 5:8)

The context surrounding the statement makes its meaning very clear. "But do not," wrote Paul, "let immorality or any impurity or greed even be named among you, as is proper among saints; and there must be no filthiness and silly talk, no coarse jesting, which are not fitting, but rather giving of thanks. ... And do not participate in the unfruitful deeds of darkness, but instead even expose them; for it is disgraceful even to speak of the things which are done by them in secret. But all things become visible when they are exposed by the *light*, for everything that becomes visible is light" (Eph. 5:3,4,11–13, italics added).

"To walk before God and be blameless" meant walking in the light. This lesson Abraham was learning, and with each new revelation from God, he took another step of obedience.

"Therefore, be careful how you walk" (Eph. 5:15)

And again, the context explains Paul's concern. To "walk carefully" means living, "not as unwise men, but as wise." It means "making the most of your time." In essence, it means "understand what the will of the Lord is" (Eph. 5:15–17).

Abraham was learning to understand God's will. What he thought was a "wise" maneuver—and may have been by pagan standards—turned out to be very unwise. What appeared to Abraham as a "time-saving" approach to the problem cost him dearly in time and effort in trying to solve the family problems he created with the birth of Ishmael.

But most important, Abraham responded to God's discipline. He was learning with every step in his life how to walk in God's will. Unlike some of us, he did not blame God and others for the mess he created. Humanly speaking, he could have been greatly tempted to blame Sarah, Hagar or even Ishmael. Furthermore, he could have been angry toward God for not being more specific in His previous revelations. But he was not. Rather, he blamed himself—for he knew he had failed God—and then he proceeded to correct the problem.

A TWENTIETH-CENTURY PERSPECTIVE

Many Christians today misunderstand the concept of the silence of God. On one hand, God has been silent most of history. On the other hand, He has *never* been silent, especially since He has revealed Himself in the Scriptures.

1. *On God's Silence*

Let me explain. The periods of time when God revealed Himself directly to men were relatively few, compared with all of history. The extent of His revelations varied and the phenomena surrounding these events also varied. Abraham, as we've seen, actually talked with God. He heard His voice, and actually saw some kind of visible manifestation.

But there were three significant periods of time when God revealed Himself to men in extensive and supernatural ways: during the last 40 years of Moses' life; during the lifetimes of Elijah and Elisha; and during the life of Christ and, briefly, following Christ's ascent to heaven. At the most, these periods of time probably do not total more than 120 to 130 years. During these periods God spoke dramatically through miracles and supernatural phenomena that revealed His great and mighty power and confirmed His written revelation to men. But between these brief periods of time, there were many silent years. In fact, God's speaking to Zechariah through the angel Gabriel about the birth of John the Baptist was probably the first time God had spoken directly to any man for 400 years.

So God has been silent for most of mankind's existence. Some Christians make a serious mistake trying to duplicate in their own lives the events and experiences of God's children who lived during these very real, but relatively brief periods of biblical history. Consequently, inner experiences and psychological feelings are often equated with the Holy Spirit, which leads to all kinds of spiritual and emotional confusion in doing the will of God.

When a Christian has a proper perspective on biblical history and on God's ways of revealing Himself, he can then understand more clearly the tendency in Christian groups today to place more emphasis on personal experience than on the Word of God. This tendency can lead to all kinds of self-deception, even causing a person to believe he is experiencing a true biblical phenomenon, when in reality it is only a psychological and physical simulation.

This is why Christians today must rely primarily on God's written revelation, the Bible, to determine the will of God. We must carefully test all experience with Scripture. And this leads us to our second perspective.

2. *On God's written revelation*

From one perspective, then, God has been silent for most of man's existence. On the other hand, God has never been silent. Paul reminds us in Romans that "since the creation of the world His invisible attributes, His eternal power and divine nature, have been clearly seen, being understood through what has been made, so that they are without excuse" (Rom. 1:20).

It is also true that apart from God's written revelation we would know nothing of His redemptive plan in Jesus Christ. His oral messages to both Old Testament and New Testament prophets would be clearly lost or terribly twisted had they not been recorded. From the time the Scriptures were supernaturally inspired, we have an accurate account of God's great plan for men. In this sense, He is still speaking today. What He said dramatically and directly to the prophets, often accompanied with miraculous signs, is just as true as we read it today as it was the moment it was written down.

3. *On knowing the will of God*

Every Christian who has access to the Bible has a far greater advantage in being able to know God's will than Abraham. The letter to the Ephesian Christians alone gives us a far greater perspective on the will of God than Abraham ever had.

In addition to the lessons that emerge from Abraham's life, we have those from many other biblical characters. The Ephesian letter is only one of many that gives us specific directions in knowing God's will.

In the Word of God we have everything we need to know to avoid serious mistakes in discovering His will. A Christian who studies the Scriptures, applies their principles, and obeys their commands will have little difficulty determining what God wants him to do. Where to go to school, choosing a vocation, dating and marriage, undertaking business ventures—all these fall naturally in place when we obey God's specific will as revealed in the Scriptures. We need not fear a 13-year mistake like Abraham made. There is no reason why it

111

should ever happen—unless we fail to study and obey the written Word of God.

LIFE RESPONSE

Following are the five basic directives that Paul gave the Ephesian Christians regarding the will of God. To what extent are you satisfied that you are obeying God and living up to the light you have?

1. I am walking in a manner worthy of the calling with which I have been called (Eph. 4:1).

   Dissatisfied   1   2   3   4   5   Satisfied

2. I am not walking any longer the way Gentiles (or non-Christians) walk (Eph. 4:17).

   Dissatisfied   1   2   3   4   5   Satisfied

3. I am walking in love, as Christ loved me (Eph. 5:1).

   Dissatisfied   1   2   3   4   5   Satisfied

4. I am walking in the light (Eph. 5:8).

   Dissatisfied   1   2   3   4   5   Satisfied

5. I am walking carefully, making the most of my time, understanding what God's will is (Eph. 5:15–17).

   Dissatisfied   1   2   3   4   5   Satisfied

FAMILY OR GROUP PROJECT

Study carefully Romans 12:1,2. How do these verses correlate with Paul's exhortations to the Ephesian Christians? In what ways can we apply these truths to our day-by-day Christian living in the decisions we make?

Footnote

1. F.B. Meyer, *Abraham*, p. 102.

10

SARAH'S UNBELIEF AND GOD'S RESPONSE

*And we are sure of this, that he will listen to us when-
ever we ask Him for anything in line with his will. And
if we really know he is listening when we talk to him and
make our requests, then we can be sure that he will
answer us.*

1 John 5:14,15, TLB

When you look at the whole biblical story of Abraham
and see it unfold chapter by chapter, it is not difficult to
sense the emotional anxiety and bitterness Sarah must
have experienced. Up to this time Sarah had not heard
God speak; she only had Abraham's report about his
conversations with God. Yet all through the years she
had faithfully followed Abraham as he followed God.

The following dialogue, of course, is fictional. But this
could have been the way Sarah reacted the day Abraham tried to tell her about their coming blessed event:

SARAH: Nonsense, Abraham! You've had another
one of those hallucinations. I really thought you were

over those problems. It's been 13 years since you thought you heard God's voice. I really think your "conversations" with God have been in your imagination all along.

ABRAHAM: I know it's hard to believe, Sarah, but I saw Him. I saw God! And I did hear His voice. It was no hallucination.

SARAH: Well, what do you *think* He said this time?

ABRAHAM: We made a mistake, Sarah. A bad mistake! I should never have tried to produce a child by Hagar. God has told me very clearly that you are supposed to be the mother of my son—of the promised seed.

SARAH: ME? Now I know you're crazy, Abraham. You know I can't bear children. I never have been able to. And even 13 years ago it would have been impossible.

ABRAHAM: That's where we made our mistake. It's *not* impossible with God. He is God Almighty. He can make it possible—even right now!

SARAH: (Shaking head) Abraham, have you lost your senses completely? You've even forgotten how old I am! And look at you!

ABRAHAM: You are 90 years old, Sarah! And I am 99. I know that! And so does God. In fact, that's been part of His plan all along. Our son is to be a miracle child, a child born in our old age.

SARAH: How do you know that?

ABRAHAM: God told me.

SARAH: God told you! God told you! Abraham, I'm fed up with this whole thing. I tried to help God out. And I tried to help you out. Remember? I gave you Hagar, my own personal slave, into your arms. And what did I get? When she became pregnant, she made fun of me. She laughed at me. And when I drove her out—with *your* permission, Abraham—God appeared

114

to *her* and sent her back with that wild kid of yours. (Pause) You know, Abraham, I'll bet she made that whole story up! God didn't appear to her! She just wanted back in our household! Why, I'd like to—

ABRAHAM: (Speaking in a very comforting but firm fashion) Sarah! Sarah!

SARAH: (Sarah breaks down, with a pause) I'm sorry, Abraham. I'm so confused. I meant well. But it just didn't turn out right. I guess I'm terribly bitter.

ABRAHAM: (Tenderly, holding Sarah, pausing until weeping subsides) I know how you feel. It's been a rough 13 years for all of us. But God hasn't forsaken us, Sarah. I just misunderstood Him. It's mostly my fault, not yours, that all of this has happened.

SARAH: I *want to believe you*, Abraham! I want to believe that God really will work a miracle. But—right now— (Pause) I just can't!

Sarah still was not convinced that she could bear a child in her old age. And her skepticism was understandable. Remember, she had never heard God speak directly to her. God had always appeared and spoken to Abraham, never to her.

Yet Sarah really meant well, even when she gave Hagar to Abraham. Then, when the whole plan backfired and God actually spoke directly *to* Hagar rather than *to* her, she must have suffered all kinds of negative feelings—jealousy, bitterness and emotional confusion. After all, Sarah was a human being, too, and no doubt quite carnal in her whole outlook on life.

Of course, God knew all this. He was working in Sarah's life just as He was in Abraham's. He was just as concerned with Sarah. She was just as important in God's plan as Abraham, for she was to be the mother of the promised seed. But Abraham was having difficulty communicating this message to Sarah.

GOD'S APPEARANCE TO ABRAHAM AND
HIS EAGER RESPONSE (Gen. 18:1–8)

What was Abraham to do? He faced another dilemma. *He* believed God, but *his wife didn't!* How could he convince Sarah that God meant what He said?

Abraham had learned his lesson well. By faith he waited on God to help him solve his communication problem with Sarah. Of course, there wasn't much else he could do. He had to turn the problem completely over to God. By this time, being 99 years old, Abraham was himself too old to produce a child. He could only wait for a total miracle.

Abraham waited—with an expectant heart. And God did not disappoint him. He "appeared to him by the oaks of Mamre, while he was sitting at the tent door in the heat of the day" (18:1). There were actually three men who appeared, but Abraham recognized one of them immediately: He was God in the form of a man.

Abraham's response was more than an act of Eastern hospitality. Though "running" to meet a stranger and "bowing low" to greet him was not an unusual practice in those days, it seems there was an element of expectation and excitement in Abraham's behavior toward these three visitors that surpassed common courtesy. "My Lord," he pleaded, directing his request to the stranger who stood among the trees, "if now I have found favor in your sight, please do not pass your servant by" (18:3).

Abraham had been waiting for this moment—this moment when he would encounter the Lord again. It would not be surprising to someday learn, when talking with Abraham in heaven, that he had been crying out to God in prayer, seeking His help in his present dilemma. The Lord's sudden appearance didn't seem to catch Abraham totally off guard. He responded as if he had been expecting another message from God.

116

Abraham's tactic in getting these three men to stay with them for a period of time is really quite human—and humorous. Inwardly, the Lord Himself must have been smiling when Abraham invited them to stay for a "piece of bread" and then hastened to kill the fatted calf (18:4–8). Once he obtained a commitment from them to remain for a snack, Abraham personally supervised the preparation of a fantastic feast. What turned out to be an invitation for "hamburgers" turned out, by design, to be a steak dinner with all the trimmings.

The text speaks for itself: "So Abraham hurried into the tent to Sarah, and said, 'Quickly, prepare three measures of fine flour, knead it, and make bread cakes.' Abraham also ran to the herd, and took a tender and choice calf, and gave it to the servant; and he hurried to prepare it. And he took curds and milk and the calf which he had prepared, and placed it before them; and he was standing by them under the tree as they ate" (18:6–8).

Abraham knew he was entertaining the God of heaven. He knew that God Almighty was the only One who could solve his family problems and fulfill His promise of an eternal seed. Following the meal, the Lord turned His attention to the primary reason He had appeared to Abraham by the Oaks of Mamre.

GOD'S FIRST MESSAGE TO SARAH AND HER INITIAL RESPONSE (Gen. 18:9–12)

At the right moment, knowing that Sarah was sitting behind a thin curtain of camel's hair inside her tent, and all ears, the three men posed a question: "Where is Sarah your wife?" (18:9). And then for her benefit, the Lord repeated His promise to Abraham in her hearing: "I will surely return to you at this time next year; and behold, Sarah your wife shall have a son" (18:10).

Can you imagine Sarah's response when she suddenly

heard her name? The Lord's message to her, though indirect because it was spoken to Abraham, still came through loud and clear. The Lord got her attention. She "was listening at the tent door." But her reaction was not positive. When she heard the Lord's words, she "laughed to herself, saying, 'After I have become old, shall I have pleasure, my lord being old also?'" (18:12).

Sarah's response of doubt and pessimism set the stage for God's second message to Sarah, one that jolted her and caused her to do some very serious thinking.

GOD'S SECOND MESSAGE TO SARAH AND HER ULTIMATE RESPONSE (Gen. 18:13–15; Heb. 11:11,12)

Sarah's laugh was "within herself." It was not audible to human ears. And the curtain of camel's hair hid any negative expressions that may have appeared on her countenance. Imagine her total surprise when the Lord immediately asked Abraham a question: "Why did Sarah laugh?" (18:13).

And the second question that the Lord raised in her hearing must have pierced deeply into Sarah's heart and soul: "Is anything too difficult for the Lord?" (18:14).

What a gracious and beautiful technique! The Lord, in the very process of communicating about the miracle He would perform, actually performed a miracle. He read Sarah's mind. Without having heard or seen her, He exposed the innermost thoughts and feelings of her heart. You see, God was teaching Sarah the same lesson He had just taught Abraham—that He was the Almighty God and that He could do anything, even that which is against nature.

This is the very same approach Jesus Christ used with Thomas, the doubting apostle. After His resurrection, Christ had appeared to the other disciples. But Thomas was not there. And when they reported they had seen the Lord, Thomas responded with bold words of unbelief: "Unless I shall see in His hands the imprint of the nails, and put my finger into the place of the nails, and put my hand into His side, I will not believe" (John 20:25).

Eight days following this negative reaction, the Lord once again appeared to His disciples—and this time Thomas was there. Without any communication, without any report from the other apostles regarding the specific content of Thomas' statement, Jesus immediately walked over to Thomas and said, "Reach here your finger, and see My hands; and reach here your hand, and put it into My side; and be not unbelieving, but believing" (John 20:27).

Thomas' response was immediate and dramatic: "My Lord and My God!" (John 20:28). Jesus had repeated the very words that Thomas had spoken to the other disciples, and without being there to hear what he had said. And Thomas recognized the miracle.

The Lord's message to Sarah was just as dramatic, perhaps more so. In her case there was no audible verbalization, only inner thoughts. Yet God's response was immediate—instantaneous.

Sarah's response, however, was not positive, as was that of Thomas. In fact, her immediate and initial response was negative and defensive. In fear, she lied and denied she had laughed. But God's response was just as immediate: "No, but you *did* laugh" (Gen. 18:15, italics added).

How long it took Sarah to overcome her embarrassment, to lower her defenses, to admit her bitterness, fear and unbelief, we do not know. But we do know that she ultimately did respond. For in the book of Hebrews we read, "By faith even Sarah herself received ability to conceive, even beyond the proper time of life, since she considered Him faithful who had promised" (Heb. 11: 11).

GOD'S RESPONSE TO MAN TODAY

Is God the same today as He was in Abraham's day? Can He work the same miracles? The answer, of course, is a decided yes! He is just as capable of doing anything He wants to today as He was before. *Nothing* is too difficult for the Lord. He is still omnipotent. In His essential nature He is immutable. He is the same yesterday, today and forever (Heb. 13:8).

But this does not mean that God always does things the same way. Throughout the Bible, our only inerrant and totally accurate account of God's dealing with mankind, we see a variation in the manifestation of God's miraculous power. Sometimes it was in response to specific prayer, and sometimes it was a sovereign act of God apart from man's desires or will.

For example, God on occasions would open the womb of a woman who could not bear children. Sarah, of course, was such a person, and an exception in Scripture since she was 90 years old. Hannah was another such person when she conceived and gave birth to Samuel (1 Sam. 1:1–20).

And Mary, the mother of Jesus, stands out as a person involved in one of God's greatest miracles. She actually conceived a child without natural means. And interestingly, the words to Mary by the angel Gabriel were almost identical in meaning to God's words to Sarah that day near the Oaks of Mamre:

To Sarah God said, "Is anything too difficult for the Lord?" (Gen. 18:14). The answer, of course, was no!

And to Mary, God put both the question and the answer together in one profound and startling statement: "For nothing will be impossible with God" (Luke 1:37).

It is important to realize, however, that these events were not the norm. They were exceptions in God's plan. God performed these miracles *when* He wanted to and

120

in His own sovereign way. But the fact that He doesn't do it every day doesn't mean that He cannot. This is true of every miracle that is recorded in the Bible. God could repeat them all any time, any place and in the life of any person He chose.

What then can we expect God to do today? How does He respond to our prayers in the twentieth century?

The whole of Scripture yields some dynamic guidelines and principles for answering these questions:

1. *We must acknowledge that on this earth we will never understand completely the way God works in our Christian lives.* His will and ways are so far beyond ours that we can only catch a small glimpse of His fathomless personality. Paul expressed it well in his Roman letter: "Oh the depth of the riches both of the wisdom and knowledge of God! How unsearchable are His judgments and unfathomable His ways! For who has known the mind of the Lord, or who became His counselor? Or who has first given to Him that it might be paid back to Him again? For from Him and through Him and to Him are all things. To Him be the glory forever. Amen" (Rom. 11:33–36).

In the Old Testament, the prophet Isaiah captured the same truth: " 'For My thoughts are not your thoughts, neither are your ways My ways,' declares the Lord. 'For as the heavens are higher than the earth, so are My ways higher than your ways, and My thoughts than your thoughts' " (Isa. 55:8,9).

So as Christians we must not be confused and disillusioned if there are aspects of God's dealings with us that we cannot understand. But on the other hand, the Scriptures *do* give us sufficient insight into God's mind and plan for us to be comfortable in our Christian lives and to understand His ways enough that we can pray to Him regarding our human predicaments. And this leads us to a second guideline or principle.

121

2. *God's response to twentieth-century man is always according to His will.* So we must pray according to His will. The apostle John wrote, "And this is the confidence which we have before Him, that, if we ask anything according to His will, He hears us" (1 John 5:14).

The next question, of course, is how do we know how to pray according to His will? There is only one solution to that problem. God's will is recorded in the Scriptures —His special revelation to help us discover His plan for mankind.

I need not pray, "Lord, if it is your will, heal this marriage." I already know it is His will that a marriage be restored. God has clearly and succinctly said without qualifications, "What therefore God has joined together, let no man separate" (Matt. 19:6).

On the other hand, I cannot pray, "Lord, heal this person from his brain tumor," for nowhere in the Bible am I told that God will heal all physical (or even emotional) sickness. Yet according to the Scriptures I can always pray confidently: "Lord, if it is your will, heal this person."

Sometimes God answers these prayers. Sometimes, in His sovereign will, He does not. But whether He answers specifically or not, He always wants us to pray. And for the most part, when He responds, He responds to specific prayers.

3. *God is sovereign but He honors man's will.* He does not force people to do something they do not want to do. I can pray, "Lord, change that person's bitter attitude"—and I need not pray, "if it be your will." I already know that it is His will that no Christian be bitter (see Eph. 4:31,32). But if a person chooses to be bitter, God will not force that person to be loving.

We must remember, too, that God may choose to answer our prayer by using us to confront that person with his bitterness. In fact, it is God's will that we ap-

122

proach him lovingly, and directly make him aware of his specific problem. But we have no guarantee that he will respond. For God has chosen not to violate any person's will, even though He could do so.

God has put the responsibility for response on each of us. True, God will lovingly discipline His child as a means to draw him back into His will (see Heb. 12:7,8), but some Christians will not even respond to God's discipline. They choose to go their own way and ultimately will pay the consequences.

4. *We know God responds to prayer, but we must also realize that certain promises in the Bible were spoken to certain people who lived in certain times and who were called to accomplish certain purposes.* We must always consider the context of these promises. For example, numerous prayers for dramatic healings were answered for the apostles because God chose to work miracles through them. And they knew it was His will to do so, because God had told them. In faith, they claimed His specific promises and God answered their prayers (John 14:12–14).

5. *We know the Scriptures promise overall that God hears and answers prayer.* He wants all Christians to pray regularly (1 Thess. 5:17). He wants us to pray in faith (Jas. 1:5–8). He wants us to pray persistently (Luke 18:1–8). He wants us to pray both corporately and privately, and He wants us to pray out of pure hearts. In fact, David said, "If I regard wickedness in my heart, the Lord will not hear" (Ps. 66:18).

LIFE RESPONSE

The following statements will help you evaluate your perspective on God's power, as well as your view of prayer. Isolate the factors that may be interfering with your relationship with God.

☐ There is definite sin in my life which may be keeping

God from answering my prayers. *Note:* Christian husbands, notice what God says about this in relationship to your wives—"You husbands, likewise, live with your wives in an understanding way, as with a weaker vessel, since she is a woman; and grant her honor as a fellow-heir of the grace of life so that *your prayers may not be hindered*" (1 Pet. 3:7, italics added).

☐ I do not pray regularly and specifically, which may be the reason I experience little of God's power in my life.

☐ I have a false view of God in that I try to manipulate Him to do what I want rather than what He wills.

☐ I know so little of Scripture that I have difficulty praying in His will.

☐ I am not persistent in prayer.

☐ Other _____

_____

FAMILY OR GROUP PROJECT

Review this chapter and then discuss the Life Response. Be specific. What can you do as a family or overall group, or as an individual, to become more faithful in prayer in discovering God's power?

11

A CASE OF
MIXED EMOTIONS

He walked away, perhaps a stone's throw, and knelt down and prayed this prayer: "Father, if you are willing, please take away this cup of horror from me. But I want your will, not mine."

Luke 22:41,42, TLB

Is it possible for a child of God to be in the "good and acceptable and perfect" will of God (Rom. 12:1,2) and yet experience negative emotions and difficult problems? More specifically, is it possible to have negative experiences because you are actually doing God's will?

The answer, of course, is a decided yes!

Isaac's birth demonstrates this reality. At first, Abraham and Sarah experienced happiness and great joy. But later, some negative feelings and responses emerged and mingled with these positive feelings, causing ambivalence and mixed emotions.

Why did this happen? What transpired? When you understand the dynamics of being human, when you face the realities of sin, when you acknowledge the lingering effects of failure and when you see the specific events in Abraham's and Sarah's lives in total perspective, it is not difficult to understand their mixed emotions. Abraham and Sarah were human, as we are. They faced ambivalence and mixed feelings in doing the will of God, as do all Christians.

ISAAC'S BIRTH (Gen. 21:1–5)

That day, that moment, finally arrived. God's promise to Abraham and Sarah became a living reality. For years they had waited—at times doubting, at times confused, at times attempting to take matters into their own hands. But when God was ready, when the time was right, He "took note of Sarah as He had said, and the Lord did for Sarah as He had promised" (21:1).

God's promise fulfilled

God exists as the Almighty God! He is omnipotent and all powerful! But one thing He cannot do, nor would He do if He could: He cannot lie! When He makes a promise, He will never break it.

Paul, writing to Titus of God's promise regarding the future state of a Christian, said without equivocation; "In the hope of eternal life, which God, who cannot lie, promised long ages ago" (Titus 1:2). God's promise to Abraham and Sarah embraces the great salvation plan that Paul was writing about. You see, God's initial promise of a son to Abraham when he was yet in Ur included a blessing for all families of the earth (Gen. 12:3)—the blessing of salvation through Jesus Christ. For Christ Himself was indeed of the seed of Abraham.

It's not surprising, then, that Paul also wrote to the Galatian Christians, "When the fulness of the time came, God sent forth His Son, born of a woman" (Gal. 4:4). This fulfillment constitutes an extension of God's promise to Abraham and Sarah, for it was also in the fullness of time that Isaac was born. From God's perspective, the promised seed was right on schedule!

126

"Sarah conceived and bore a son to Abraham in his old age, at the appointed time of which God had spoken to him" (Gen. 21:2).

Abraham's obedience

Abraham immediately named his son Isaac, which means "he laughs." Abraham was obeying God, for the Lord had actually named Isaac before his birth. In a previous encounter with Abraham, God had informed him that Sarah, not Hagar, would bear the promised seed. Abraham, nonplussed and confused, "fell on his face and laughed" and begged that "Ishmael might live" before God (Gen. 17:17,18). God's response was quick and unmoving—"No, but Sarah your wife shall bear you a son, and you shall call his name Isaac" (Gen. 17:19).

The name Isaac was to stand out on the pages of history as a constant reminder to the world that, on the one hand, God's promises are no laughing matter. On the other hand, this was a promise that *was* going to be a "laughing matter"—a hilarious event because of its impossibility from a human perspective.

Abraham also obeyed God by circumcising his son "when he was eight days old" (Gen. 21:4). This was God's command to Abraham and His covenant with him (Gen. 17:7–14). There is no doubt that Abraham was responding to the will of God. He wanted no other way but God's way!

POSITIVE RESPONSES TO ISAAC'S BIRTH
(Gen. 21:6–8)

Imagine the reaction Isaac's birth must have had on all those who heard about it. Abraham had many servants, as we read in Genesis 13 and 14. What was their response when they heard that a 90-year-old woman had given birth to a son? What was the response of the other people who lived in Kadesh and Shur, those under the rule of Abimelech? We can only wonder. But the Scriptures tell us clearly the response of Sarah and Abraham.

Sarah's joy

"God has made laughter for me," Sarah proclaimed when Isaac was born. And "everyone who hears will laugh with me" (21:6). Here is true biblical laughter. Here is true joy.

What a contrast to Sarah's previous response when God told her she would have a son in her old age. Inwardly, she had laughed—an expression of unbelief. To her it was impossible. Then, it had been a laugh of doubt and of skepticism! (Gen. 18:12).

But now, on the day Isaac was born, her laugh was one of rejoicing and happiness. The baby was real! In her arms and on her breast was the little son God had promised. It was no longer a dream or a figment of someone's imagination.

What made the event so hilarious was the fact that Sarah was a very old woman and Abraham was a very old man. But in spite of their age, together they had produced a child. To her and to every onlooker, it was really a laughing matter. She must have chuckled (no longer inwardly, but for all to hear), as she queried: "Who would have said to Abraham that Sarah would nurse children? Yet I have borne him a son in his old age" (21:7).

Abraham's feast

Abraham's response was also very positive, even perhaps more so than Sarah's. Before him was the child who had been promised by God ever since the Lord first appeared to him in Ur. And in true Eastern tradition, Abraham planned "a great feast on the day that Isaac was weaned" (21:8), probably when he was three, or perhaps four years old. It was a great occasion, with more than the usual significance. For at this time, Abraham no doubt announced for all to hear that before them stood the promised seed, the one through whom God would produce "a great nation"; the one who would make Abraham's "name great"; the one in whom "all the families of the earth shall be blessed" (Gen. 12:2, 3).

NEGATIVE RESPONSES TO ISAAC'S BIRTH
(Gen. 21:9–14)

What was a great joyous occasion soon created some very negative reactions and feelings. First it was Ishmael, then Sarah and finally Abraham.

Ishmael's ridicule

By now, Ishmael was probably 16 or 17 years old. As a growing and alert teenager, he in no way would miss the message he was hearing. The lad had often been told by his parents that he was the promised seed and now he gradually began to realize that his folks were in error. They had deceived him as well as themselves.

Bitterness and anger began to well up within Ishmael as Isaac, little by little, began to replace him. And no doubt, the great feast and the glad speeches in Isaac's honor caused these feelings of bitterness to reflect themselves in ridicule and mockery (Gen. 21:9). What he did and how he did it, we can only conjecture. But one thing is sure. Ishmael's jealousy had turned into mockery.

Sarah's resentment

Whatever Ishmael did and whatever he said, quickly revived in Sarah the old feelings of bitterness and anger she had toward Hagar and her son. Quickly she reverted to old emotional patterns and reactions, a desire to rid her household of this slave girl and the son she had borne Abraham (Gen. 16:6; 21:10).

129

How frequently over the years Sarah must have been reminded of Hagar's attitudes toward her. How much she must have struggled with her feelings of resentment and bitterness. And how true this is of so many of us. Once we become bitter toward someone, it takes very little stimulus to generate those feelings again. They seem to lie buried just below the surface, ready to erupt at the slightest provocation. We're always vulnerable toward that person, particularly when he is a member of our family.

Sarah was no exception. She was *very* human! And in this human predicament she reacted with all of her humanness. Earlier it had been Hagar who had despised Sarah. Now it was Ishmael who ridiculed Isaac. But the same people were involved. Consequently, the negative emotions and reactions were predictable.

Abraham's remorse

No doubt Abraham thought that the past was dead and buried, that his mistake was forgotten. But how quickly he discovered that it was only suppressed in Sarah's memory and very much alive. When Sarah came running to Abraham, demanding that he "drive out this maid and her son," he was greatly distressed (Gen. 21: 10,11). He was grief-stricken, depressed and once again filled with remorse. Wouldn't the past ever go away?

But at this point, though Abraham responded to the matter with emotional stress and anxiety—and who wouldn't?—he *acted* maturely. Previously, he had copped out as head of the household and quickly placed the burden back on Sarah (Gen. 16:6). He would not face the responsibility for his own mistake.

But this time, rather than taking Sarah's advice, he faced the problem squarely and waited on the Lord for a solution. And God did not forsake him. For in time, the Lord appeared to Abraham with a direct and con-

130

firming message: "Do not be distressed because of the lad and your maid; whatever Sarah tells you, listen to her, for through Isaac your descendants shall be named" (21:12).

Though Sarah had spoken out of deep feelings of resentment and bitterness, what she said this time was according to the will of God.

God also put Abraham's heart at ease about Hagar and Ishmael. Abraham no doubt still had deep feelings of appreciation for Hagar and especially for her son. He had weathered some very difficult years with Ishmael, teaching him, training him and learning to appreciate his wild and determined spirit. Like a young and frisky colt who has won the heart of his master, so Ishmael had a deep place in the heart of his father.

God's sympathy was with Abraham. He understood his agony and distress. Consequently, He reassured Abraham that He would take care of Hagar and Ishmael. "Because he is your descendant," said the Lord, "I will make [him] a nation also" (21:13).

And God did. He delivered the bondmaid and her son from death in the desert. And eventually Ishmael married a girl from his mother's country, the land of Egypt. And from this union came a great nation—millions of people who to this day occupy the great Arab countries of the world.

AMBIVALENCE TODAY

Unfortunately, some Christians believe that being in the will of God will solve all of their problems. They expect no more anxiety, no more stress, no more breakdowns in communication, no more difficult situations. This, of course, is not a true perspective on life, even a life lived in obedience to God.

Abraham's experience following the birth of Isaac teaches us a dynamic lesson. There is no doubt that he was in the perfect will of God. He had produced the promised seed by Sarah. He named him Isaac as God had said. He circumcised him on the eighth day. In grand fashion he prepared a feast and proclaimed to others that Isaac was the child of promise.

What more could Abraham have done to demonstrate his desire to do God's will? As far as we can tell from Scripture, the answer is "nothing." Why, then, did he have to face the distress and depression caused by Ishmael's ridicule and Sarah's hostility? Why wasn't he able to "live happily ever after," rejoicing in the fulfilled promise of God?

There are two basic answers to these questions:

We reap what we sow

Abraham was experiencing the results of his previous mistake. He had definitely violated God's will in having a child by Hagar, even though he thought he was helping God out. It was Sarah's idea, but it created bitterness in her and eventually jealousy in Ishmael. There was no way to avoid the aftermath of this problem. In the words of Paul, *Abraham was reaping* what he had sown (see Gal. 6:7). Certain mistakes tend to rise and haunt us. And this was one of them.

A specific lesson for most Christians that emerges from Abraham's life is that very few of us are exempt from suffering as a result of our sinful past. We are still periodically haunted today by our past. Sometime, somewhere, and under certain conditions, we will remember our mistake and experience anxiety and stress. And sometimes it jolts us pretty hard, like it did Abraham. When everything is going so well, we think our error has been forgotten. But suddenly, there it looms before us, in all of its ugliness, creating all kinds of emotional ambivalence in us and others.

Another lesson from Abraham's life is seen in his

response. True, he was depressed; he experienced remorse; he was emotionally upset. But he reacted in a mature fashion.

Abraham consulted the Lord. He waited until he had a clear perspective on the problem. Then he faced reality and did what he had to do.

In this case, *Abraham was able,* in the will of God, *to remove the cause of the problem.* And in our lives sometimes this is also a possibility. When it is, we must take steps to root out the problem.

But in other circumstances it may not be possible without committing another wrong. And two wrongs never make a right. We may have to live with the situation, attempting to do the will of God in spite of our mistakes. And, of course, our only guideline for what is right and what is wrong, what we can remove and what we cannot remove, comes to us from God's Word.

So, if you are a human being, face the fact that because you are, you have no doubt done things that will create problems in the future, even though you are faithfully obeying God and following His will today. But when problems arise, remember Abraham. Consult God's Word. Remember first that God forgives the past. Then face the problem head on. Change what you can, and then learn to live with what you cannot change.

We live in a world of sin

A second answer to why Christians face problems, even when they are doing God's will, is that we live in a world contaminated by sin. Those who hate God's ways and His standards will often hate us. For example, some Christians have jobs in certain enterprises where cheating and dishonesty run rampant. If the Christian is honest, he will actually make other people look bad. A Christian in this situation who wants to please God and do His will cannot compromise his convictions.

What are the results? Frequently, the Christian is rejected. He may even be falsely accused and lose his job. He may have to live with anxiety day after day. Some Christians, unfortunately, have compromised and have faced the nagging problem of a guilty conscience, knowing they are outside of the will of God.

A dedicated Christian living in a world of sin has no guarantee that his life will be one of total peace and inner harmony. In fact, sometimes to choose to do God's will brings extreme frustration and stress. But on the other hand, a Christian who knows he is doing the will of God in spite of persecution and rejection will have the deep-settled peace and satisfaction that he is pleasing God rather than men.

We must point out, of course, that some Christians get themselves into trouble because they are insensitive and unwise in their dealings with non-Christians. Here Paul had something to say, as he spoke to the Philippian Christians who were serving non-Christian masters: "Do all things without grumbling or disputing; that you may prove yourselves to be blameless and innocent, children of God above reproach in the midst of a crooked and perverse generation, among whom you appear as lights in the world" (Phil. 2:14,15).

The Christian must do all he can to do a good job, but he must never purposely put other people down and make them look bad. In his decisions not to compromise, he should remember the words of Jesus Christ, who said: "Behold, I send you out as sheep in the midst of wolves; therefore be shrewd as serpents, and innocent as doves" (Matt. 10:16).

LIFE RESPONSE

What is the reason for *your* ambivalence, *your* emotional pain—even though you are trying to do God's will? Is it because of past mistakes—in your family, at work, with friends? Or is it because you are simply living for God in a sinful world? Whatever the source, the following realizations will help you face your situation:

1. If I am plagued by a past mistake, first of all, *I accept total forgiveness in Jesus Christ.* I confess my sin, and I believe that God has forgiven me (see 1 John 1:9).

2. *I know, however, that forgiveness from God does not do away with the result of some mistakes.* First, I will face the reality of the past and its influence on the present; secondly, I will respond maturely to the problem, doing what I can to change the situation and learning to live with what I cannot change.

Note: There are few situations that cannot be changed, at least to a certain extent, in order to ease the problem of stress and anxiety.

3. *I also realize that just doing the will of God in a sinful world will bring a certain degree of emotional, and perhaps even physical, pain.* I will first of all make sure I am not suffering unnecessarily because of unwise behavior on my part. And second, if the problems are unavoidable, I will do what I can to live for Jesus Christ in spite of the problems, even if it means personal loss and rejection.

And now, from these general statements, what *specific* problems are you facing? And what are you going to do about it? Be specific. _____

_____

FAMILY OR GROUP PROJECT

Encourage members of your family or group to share some of the problems they are facing—in school, at work, at play—because of their desire to do the will of God. Help each other develop a biblical approach to facing and solving these problems.

12

ABRAHAM'S GREATEST TEST

Though He slay me, I will hope in Him.   *Job 13:15*

Following the distress and tension involved with sending Hagar and Ishmael away from his household, Abraham entered a period of unprecedented peace and peaceful existence. There was harmony in his family, he was at peace with his neighbors, and most significantly, his relationship with God grew deeper and more meaningful than ever before. He had no greater friend than the One he had come to know and love as the Almighty and Everlasting God (see Gen. 17:1; 21:33).

And Abraham knew no greater satisfaction and source of fulfillment than that which he found in his young son, Isaac. As they climbed the gently rolling hills surrounding Beersheba and together viewed the beautiful and productive country to the north, they often reflected on God's promise to give Isaac and his descendants that land. Isaac's youthful and expectant spirit ignited the old man's heart with intense joy and excitement. Memories often flooded his soul, memories that reminded Abraham of God's faithfulness.

But during these days and years of sunshine and shade

under his tamarisk tree in Beersheba (Gen. 21:33), little did Abraham realize that this restful experience was preparing him for a severe and sudden storm, sorrow and deep trial. It would be one of the greatest tests that any man has ever faced on earth. It is a scene in history surpassed only by one other—when "God so loved the world, that He gave His only begotten Son" to die for the sins of the world (John 3:16).

God was about to issue a command to His friend that would bring Abraham to a choice experience few men have known. On the one side stood Isaac, the child of promise; on the other side stood the God of heaven. And what God wanted Abraham to do must have initially shattered every nerve in his old and deteriorating body and stretched to the breaking point every bit of spiritual fiber in his faithful soul.

GOD'S INCONGRUOUS COMMAND (Gen. 22:1,2)

"Now it came about after these things, that God tested Abraham, and said to him, 'Abraham!' And he said, 'Here I am.' And He said, 'Take now your son, your only son, whom you love, Isaac, and go to the land of Moriah; and offer him there as a burnt offering on one of the mountains of which I will tell you' " (Gen. 22:1,2).

What God asked Abraham to do was incongruous. From every human viewpoint it was contradictory and inconsistent. God had promised Abraham that He would establish His covenant *with Isaac.* And it was to be "an everlasting covenant for his descendants after him" (Gen. 17:19).

You see, Isaac was the promised seed, the product of a miraculous conception. Abraham's future children were to come from him. And now God was asking Abraham to offer Isaac as a sacrifice, to take his life, to literally cut the life-line that would be the channel through whom God had said He would carry out His promise. There was no earthly way to harmonize God's previous promise with His present command.

And remember, from Abraham's perspective God's command was a reality. There was no indication in those initial statements from God what He would eventually do. And it *was* a command, not a request. There was no escape route. There were only two alternatives for Abraham—obedience or disobedience. And a choice to obey would mean *total obedience*, to *every word* God had spoken. And that was the choice Abraham made!

ABRAHAM'S IMMEDIATE OBEDIENCE (Gen. 22:3–10)

Though Abraham's initial reactions to God's command must have been surprise and shock, his recovery time must have been very brief. We read that he "rose early in the morning" and began the journey to carry out what God had told him to do (22:3).

What arguments or dialogue Abraham had with God that night, we do not know. In his humanness he must have questioned God's request. The incongruity of it all must have flooded his heart and soul. And the darkness of the night sky must have accentuated the darkness that shrouded his whole being. Though Abraham had no doubt witnessed on numerous occasions human sacrifice for sin on Canaanite altars, there was no way he could understand God's command to offer his own first-born. It had to be an absolute step of faith in the God who had never failed him or let him down.

Yet Abraham obeyed. By morning the issue had been settled. He had experienced the faithfulness of God too often to doubt Him now. Though he knew he had to slay his only son, the promised seed, in his heart he knew that God would yet carry out His promise. The One who cannot lie *must* have another plan.

And so for three long days, hand in hand, Abraham and Isaac journeyed toward Moriah. As they left behind the young men who had accompanied them and climbed the steep slope, Isaac's questions must have brought tears to the old man's eyes. So often he had observed his father sacrifice a lamb to the God of heaven. But this time there was no lamb.

"Behold, the fire and the wood," queried Isaac, "but where is the lamb for the burnt offering?" (22:7).

Abraham's response was quick and reassuring—"God will provide for Himself the lamb for the burnt offering, my son" (22:8).

In no way could Abraham, at this moment, explain in detail what was about to transpire. He could only protect Isaac from the fear that must have begun to grip his little heart. For Isaac, even in his brief years, must have heard about or observed firsthand the Canaanite fathers who, burdened with their sins, offered their firstborn on sacrificial altars in order to placate the pagan gods.

Could it be that his own father was about to offer him as a sacrifice to the God he loved and trusted? But why? His father and his God were friends!

Abraham's confident response must have reassured the little lad. And there *was* confidence, for Abraham knew in his heart he would once again descend the mountain, hand in hand, with his beloved son. This is why he instructed the young men accompanying him, "Stay here with the donkey, and I and the lad will go yonder; and we will worship and return to you" (22:5). Though he knew no other plan but to plunge the knife into his own flesh and blood, he believed that God was able to bring Isaac back to life. It was the only way he could reconcile God's previous promise with His present command (see Heb. 11:17–19).

GOD'S INTERVENING PROVISION (Gen. 22:11–19)

God honored Abraham's obedience and his faith. As he "stretched out his hand, and took the knife to slay his

139

son," the Lord intervened. From heaven came that familiar voice calling his name. It was the voice he had heard so often, but never had he heard such welcome words—"Do not stretch out your hand against the lad, and do nothing to him; for now I know that you fear God, since you have not withheld you son, your only son, from Me" (22:12).

From God's perspective, Abraham had already offered his son. For in that great New Testament passage on faith we read: "By faith Abraham, when he was tested, offered up Isaac. . . . He considered that God is able to raise men even from the dead" (Heb. 11:17,19). In his heart, Abraham had made the decision. He was totally willing. In God's eyes Abraham had already shed the blood of his only son. He had passed the test without taking the final exam.

The rest of the story is simply told. The words of Scripture will suffice:

"Then Abraham raised his eyes and looked, and behold, behind him a ram caught in the thicket by his horns; and Abraham went and took the ram, and offered him up for a burnt offering in the place of his son. And Abraham called the name of that place The Lord Will Provide, as it is said to this day, 'In the mount of the Lord it will be provided.' Then the angel of the Lord called to Abraham a second time from heaven, and said, 'By Myself I have sworn,' declares the Lord, 'because you have done this thing, and have not withheld your son, your only son, indeed I will greatly bless you, and I will greatly multiply your seed [descendants] as the stars of the heavens, and as the sand which is on the seashore. . . . And in your seed [descendants] all the nations of the earth shall be blessed, because you have obeyed My voice.' So Abraham returned to his young men, and they arose and went together to Beersheba; and Abraham lived at Beersheba" (22:13–19).

SOME LIFE-CHANGING OBSERVATIONS

As we reflect on this story of Abraham and Isaac, several observations stand out in bold relief—observations that in themselves become immediate lessons and principles for twentieth-century Christians.

1. *God did not tempt Abraham. Rather, He tested him.* F.B. Meyer put it well: "Satan tempts us that he may bring out all the evil that is in our hearts; God tries or tests us that He may bring out all the good."[1]

Listen also to James who confirms this idea in his epistle: "Blessed is the man who perseveres under trial; for once he has been approved, he will receive the crown of life, which the Lord has promised to those who love Him. Let no one say when he is tempted, 'I am being tempted by God'; for God cannot be tempted by evil, and He Himself does not tempt any one. But each one is tempted when he is carried away and enticed by his own lust" (Jas. 1:12–14).

True, it is sometimes difficult to differentiate between a trial from God and temptation from Satan. As with Job, sometimes these two experiences intermingle. On the one hand, Satan was trying to trip him up, to make him sin, to cause him to turn against God. On the other hand, God was refining His servant, strengthening his faith and building his character.

Joseph, too, experienced this intermingling of temptation and trial. Satan was at work through his brothers. But God was also at work, even using Joseph's brothers' evil deeds to accomplish His purposes in Joseph's life. Thus Joseph could say to them: "You meant evil against me, but God meant it for good" (Gen. 50:20).

2. *God had prepared Abraham for this trial.* It is not God's plan to sneak up on a Christian's blind side and trip him up, just to make His child fail. Rather, when God tests a man He wants him to pass. Consequently, He prepares him for the crisis. In Abraham's situation

we read: "Now it came about after these things, that God tested Abraham" (Gen. 22:1).

Prior to this great test, Abraham had experienced unprecedented spiritual growth. His household was in order. Materially he was very secure, and he was at peace with his neighbors. And Isaac, the promised son, was his pride and joy. He was very happy in doing the will of God.

There was no doubt in Abraham's mind that God was real; that He loved Abraham; that He was his Friend. God had prepared him well for this great trial. When it came, and though it was painful, Abraham passed the test—with an A plus!

This is one way we can differentiate temptation from trial. Satan hits us when we're very weak; when we're not looking. He hits below the belt. He is deceptive and deceitful. He tries to destroy us.

But God tests us in order to build us up. Though He *does* deal with our weaknesses, He prepares us for the trial. And frequently His tests come after a period of learning about Him, of successes and even rest and tranquillity. This is exactly what happened to Abraham.

3. *Abraham's test came suddenly.* Life was flowing very smoothly for this Old Testament saint when suddenly he faced the greatest test of his life. One day everything was great. The next day Abraham's whole world seemed to be totally threatened.

This is frequently the pattern God follows when He tests the Christian. When everything is going smoothly, when we've worked out our problems well at one level, God suddenly tests us to raise us to a new level of patience and endurance: "Consider it all joy, my brethren, when you encounter various trials, knowing that the testing of your faith produces endurance. And let endurance have its perfect result, that you may be perfect and complete, lacking in nothing" (Jas. 1:2,3).

We must also realize that Satan often works in a sudden and subtle way, using our moments of strength to also achieve his goals. His plan is not to build character and faith but to destroy it. Hence Paul wrote to the Corinthians: "Therefore let him who thinks he stands take heed lest he fall" (1 Cor. 10:12).

We must beware, then, that success—even God's blessing in our lives—does not cause us to be lifted up with pride and to take credit for what God has done for us. If we do, we'll become vulnerable to the wiles of Satan. But on the other hand, we must take courage, for again Paul says: "No temptation has overtaken you but such as is common to man; and God is faithful, who will not allow you to be tempted beyond what you are able; but with the temptation will provide the way of escape also, that you may be able to endure it" (1 Cor. 10:13).

4. *Abraham's trial hit him in his most sensitive area.* Abraham loved God. There is no doubt about this. He had proved his love by leaving Ur, by wandering in a strange land, by giving up Ishmael. But he also loved Isaac, the child of promise. This young lad had become the focus of his life. And this we can understand. Perhaps at this point in his life, if he were asked whom he loved more—Isaac or God—it would have been difficult to answer.

So God put him to the test, in the most emotionally sensitive area of his life. Was he willing to put his Lord before Isaac? Was he willing to obey God rather than his own desires?

Abraham passed the test. He demonstrated his supreme trust and confidence in his heavenly Father.

Today God often tests His children in their most sensitive areas. What is most important in our lives? Where does our security lie?

Don't be surprised if suddenly it appears that you are called upon to make a choice between your dearest possession and the God you also love. And at that moment you will begin to realize what *is* most important. You will begin to understand how deep your love for God really is—or isn't.

And remember, love cannot be tested by *how we feel.* It is what we are prepared *to do.* Thus Jesus said to His disciples: "If you love Me, you will keep My commandments" (John 14:15).

5. *Abraham's trial appeared incongruous and illogical.* To Abraham, God's request did not make sense. It appeared inconsistent with what God had said previously. And we can understand why.

The supreme lesson for Christians today is that we must realize constantly that we operate with limited perspective. What appears illogical to us may be very logical in God's mind. What appears to be a step backward, may ultimately be a step forward. It is at this point we must throw ourselves completely on God, trust Him with all our hearts, realizing that He does care. And someday we will understand what He is accomplishing in our lives.

6. *Abraham's trial is a dynamic illustration of God's supreme love for all mankind.* Never before and never since has God ever asked a man to do what He asked Abraham to do. For in His laws which He later gave to men, God specifically forbids human sacrifice. It is an abomination to Him.

Abraham, however, lived long before God ever said anything specific about human sacrifice. In fact, this Old Testament saint had often witnessed Canaanite fathers offering their firstborn offspring on pagan altars. It was a cardinal principle in their religion, a means of atoning for their sins.

To Abraham, then, the experience was culturally related. If pagan deities who were nonexistent demanded such love, was it asking too much for the true God of heaven to require the same? Abraham had no way of perceiving as we do the inconsistency of this request with God's nature. He only knew God had spoken; he understood the request and he proceeded to obey.

Today, because we have God's completed revelation in the Bible, we know that He would never ask any man to offer his son as a human sacrifice. But we also know that what God asked Abraham to do—then stopped him from doing—illustrates for all men everywhere the great love God has for all men.

First, we learn from this experience that the shedding of blood is absolutely essential to atone for sin (see Heb. 9:22). But we also learn that the blood of bulls and goats and even an innocent lad like Isaac can never satisfy God (see Heb. 10:4). There was only one sacrifice that could atone for man's sin—the sacrifice of God's one and only Son at Calvary. It was His shed blood that provided an atonement for all men's sins.

At Calvary there was no turning back on God's part. There was no "ram caught in the thicket" that could suddenly replace the Son of God. The knife had to fall! For without that sacrifice, no man could be saved, not even Abraham of old.

LIFE RESPONSE

Spend a few moments thinking about your love for God. How deep is it? Do you worship God because it's the thing to do? Is it a token experience of your appreciation for the blessings of life? Or do you love Him with your whole heart? Is He truly first in your life?

Put another way, what would be your reaction toward God if He were to ask for your greatest possession, that which means the most to you? How deep then would be your love? How strong would be your faith?

"Father, I am a human being. You know my weaknesses. But I truly want to pray the following prayer.

145

Help me to pray it with meaning and with a true heart."

"Take my life and let it be
    consecrated, Lord, to Thee;
Take my hands, and let them move
    at the impulse of Thy love.
Take my feet, and let them be
    swift and beautiful for Thee;
Take my voice, and let me sing,
    always, only, for my King.
Take my lips, and let them be
    filled with messages for Thee;
Take my silver and my gold,
    not a mite would I withhold.
Take my moments and my days,
    let them flow in ceaseless praise;
Take my will and make it Thine,
    it shall be no longer mine;
Take my heart, it is Thine own,
    it shall be Thy royal throne.
Take my love, my God, I pour
    at Thy feet its treasure store;
Take my self, and I will be
    ever, only, all for Thee."[2]

FAMILY OR GROUP PROJECT

Review each lesson we can learn from the story of Abraham and Isaac. Share with each other specific ways God has recently *tested* you. How has Satan used these experiences to also *tempt* you? Discuss what you feel God is trying to teach you through these various trials.

Footnotes

1. F.B. Meyer, *Abraham*, p. 168.
2. Avis B. Christiansen, 1895.

13

ABRAHAM'S REPUTATION IN THE PAGAN WORLD

*Pay all your debts except the debt of love for others—
never finish paying that! For if you love them, you will
be obeying all of God's law, fulfilling all his require-
ments.*

Romans 13:8, TLB

What did the Canaanites really think of Abraham?
What were they saying about him? For many years he
wandered in their midst, settling first in one place and
then in another, pitching his tent and then building an
altar to the Lord. Everywhere he went his huge flocks
and herds, his camels and donkeys, and his numerous
servants and maids became a conspicuous part of the
landscape of Canaan. But more important, his viewpoint
on spiritual matters caused his life-style to stand out in
bold relief.

For most of Abraham's life in this new land, little was
recorded in the book of Genesis about his reputation,
how people actually viewed this wandering pilgrim.
Then one day he faced a severe but normal crisis—the
death of his faithful wife Sarah. As we study the dynamics surrounding this experience, we gain unusual insight

into this man's reputation among his pagan friends—
insights that in turn yield some dynamic principles for
Christians who are seeking to do God's will in the twentieth-century pagan world.

Sarah died at age 127, nearly 40 years after Isaac's
birth (Gen. 23:1). Incidentally, Sarah is the only woman
in the Bible whose age is recorded—and her age was
referred to often. God wanted everyone to know the
details of her life so that all who would eventually read
the account of her experience would see God's great
power manifested in giving her a son in her old age—a
child through whom all families of the earth would be
blessed by the eventual coming of Jesus Christ, the Saviour of the world.

When Sarah died, Abraham no doubt experienced
more than the usual trauma and grief. He mourned and
wept for his faithful companion (Gen. 23:2). Throughout their many years together, facing the various vicissi-
tudes of life, they had come to have much in common.

The birth of Isaac in their old age no doubt created a
bond of companionship and fellowship known by very
few couples in their latter years. During the nearly 40
years following that great miracle, they must have often
reflected on the significant event which was destined to
affect the course of human history. It must have a been
a topic that never lost its excitement and emotion.

But the day came when Sarah died. After facing the
reality of her demise, Abraham "rose from before his
dead," and began to make preparations for her burial. At
this juncture it became very apparent that his reputation
among many of the Canaanites was above reproach.

ABRAHAM'S REPUTATION AMONG
THE SONS OF HETH (Gen. 23:3–6)

The sons of Heth were Canaanites who lived near
Hebron, the place where Sarah died. And it was to those

men that Abraham made his appeal for a place to bury his wife. "I am a stranger and sojourner among you," confessed this Old Testament saint. "Give me a burial site among you, that I may bury my dead out of my sight" (23:4).

The response of the sons of Heth was dramatic: "Hear us, my lord, you are a mighty prince among us" (23:6). Or more literally, "You are a prince of God." And with this confession they were not only acknowledging Abraham's wealth and great name, but also the God who had made him great. To them, Abraham stood out among men as one whom God had greatly favored.

And how they identified Abraham represents only one dimension of the respect for this Old Testament saint. Their specific response to his request for a grave was in some respects even more dramatic: "Bury your dead in the choicest of our graves; none of us will refuse you his grave for burying your dead" (23:6).

The total context which describes how Abraham proceeded to secure a burial place for Sarah reflects the cultural practices and courtesies of the day. But there is more here than just the normal business procedures. There is also a demonstration of the true respect the sons of Heth had for Abraham. These people show an attitude of feeling honored to have been approached with this request by this wandering shepherd. They were willing to sell their own personal graves so that Abraham would have a permanent place to bury Sarah.

At this point, we could speculate in various directions. Were these men trying to impress the God of Abraham by cooperating with His "prince" (23:6)? Did they sense that this might gain them favor in God's sight? We don't know for sure but we can safely conclude they were impressed with Abraham and they were also impressed with his God! Abraham had a good reputation among his pagan neighbors.

ABRAHAM'S REPUTATION WITH EPHRON
(Gen. 23:7–16)

Abraham seems to have had an ulterior motive when he approached the sons of Heth. He desired an audience with the ruler of the city, a man named Ephron. "So Abraham rose and bowed to the people of the land, the sons of Heth. . . . 'If it is your wish for me to bury my dead out of my sight, hear me, and approach Ephron the son of Zohar for me, that he may give me the cave of Machpelah which he owns, which is at the end of his field; for the full price let him give it to me in your presence for a burial site'" (23:7–9).

Here we see Abraham's motive. He had his eye on a special cave. Often he had seen it, and must have concluded long before that this was the burial place he wanted to purchase, not only for Sarah, but also for himself (Gen. 25:9).

Ephron's response equals that of the other men. He offered Abraham not only the cave but also the field in which the cave was located (23:11). It appears he wanted to give Abraham the property at no charge.

But Abraham's response also gives us a clue as to why he was so highly respected. He refused to take the field as a gift, but insisted that he pay full market value for the piece of property. And it would be consistent with Abraham's overall life-style for us to conclude that he wanted to be obligated to no one but God.

There are several interpretations as to what transpired in this passage. Some feel Abraham was simply bartering with Ephron in order to get the cave at the proper price. If this is what happened it would certainly correlate with the cultural practices of that day. However, the total context of this chapter reflects an unusual respect for Abraham on Ephron's part, indicating that Ephron truly wanted to give Abraham the field at no extra charge.

NEW TESTAMENT CORRELATIONS

Abraham of old set a dynamic example for all Christians, both those who lived in the first century and those of us who live in today's world. He maintained a lifestyle that so impressed his pagan friends that they called him "mighty prince," literally "prince of God" (Gen. 23:6). They knew his riches came from God (and he *was* a rich man); and furthermore, Abraham made it clear throughout his life that he would do nothing to reflect negatively on the God he worshiped and served. He carefully ordered his life so that he was obligated to no one but God.

The New Testament reinforces these same basic concepts with many exhortations and references. But there are two important directives for Christians that correlate particularly with these events in Abraham's life related to Sarah's death:

First, as the apostle Paul tells us, we *"must have a good reputation with those outside the church,"* that is, with non-Christians (1 Tim. 3:7, italics added). Specifically, this is a qualification for a man who desires to be a spiritual leader in the church, but it is also the will of God for every believer.

Note what Paul wrote to other New Testament Christians:

To the Thessalonian Christians: *"Make it your ambition to lead a quiet life and attend to your own business and work with your hands,* just as we commanded you; so that you may behave properly toward outsiders and not be in any need" (1 Thess. 4:11,12, italics added).

To the Colossian Christians: *"Conduct yourselves with wisdom toward outsiders,* making the most of the opportunity. Let your speech always be with grace, seasoned, as it were, with salt, so that you may know how you should respond to each person" (Col. 4:5,6, italics added).

To the Corinthian Christians: "Whether, then, you eat or drink or *whatever you do, do all to the glory of God.* Give no offense either to Jews or to Greeks or to the church of God; just as I also please all men in all things, not seeking my own profit, but the profit of the many, that they may be saved" (1 Cor. 10:31–33, italics added).

One of the most unfortunate things that can happen to a Christian is to develop a bad reputation regarding his life-style, particularly in the way he handles money. Some Christians live above their income—and call it "living by faith." Some accumulate bills they cannot pay on time. Others let their property run down, creating resentment in their non-Christian neighbors. Some borrow money from friends and never repay them.

All of these actions bring reproach on the name of Jesus Christ and damage our Christian witness. Money is such an important part of the twentieth-century way of life, we must treat this aspect of our personal life with utmost care and diligence, guided by biblical principles.

Second, as Paul states in his letter to the Roman Christians, we *"owe nothing to anyone except to love one another"* (Rom. 13:8).

It's my personal opinion that this verse of Scripture definitely has been misinterpreted by some Christians. Some maintain that Paul was teaching that a Christian should never borrow money, never buy anything on time. And of course, it follows that it would be inconsistent for a Christian to loan money at interest. To interpret this Scripture in this way is to misapply what Paul had in mind and to ignore their culture.

What, then, does Paul mean? Paul here is saying two things:

1. *Pay your taxes.* From the context of this verse of Scripture, we know Paul is talking about a Christian's relationship to government and, specifically, he is deal-

ing with the Roman Christians' responsibility to pay taxes. Like all other citizens, the apostle exhorted them to "render to all what is due them: tax to whom tax is due; custom to whom custom; fear to whom fear; honor to whom honor" (Rom. 13:7). Paul, then, culminates this injunction with his directive, "Owe nothing to anyone except to love one another."

Paul is telling Christians, then, that we should never cheat the government. We are all to "be in subjection to the governing authorities," even though they may be non-Christians (Rom. 13:1). The only time that we are to disobey is when the government asks Christians to do something that is directly in opposition to the revealed will of God. At that juncture we must follow the example of the apostles who said on one occasion: "We must obey God rather than men" (Acts 5:29).

2. *Pay your debts.* Paul here sets forth another principle of personal fiscal responsibility that we also need to apply diligently in our present culture. But before we consider this principle in detail, let's establish what Paul *doesn't* mean when he says "owe nothing to anyone." He is not saying that a Christian should never borrow money nor lend it. Nor do his words mean that time payments are out of the will of God.

It is still possible to "owe nothing to anyone" and to have a debt, providing there is a legal agreement between the two parties. For example, when a Christian buys a house on time (about the only way the average person can buy a home), the payments are usually due at a certain time each month. Under these circumstances, an individual does not owe the loan company anything until the payment is due. However, if a person does not make his payment on time, he is in violation of Paul's injunction to "owe nothing to anyone."

On the other hand, some Christians (and most Americans) go to the opposite extreme and get caught up in

153

the credit-card craze. This approach to purchasing has become a curse to many people. What should be a Christian's perspective on what is often a "hang-loose" approach to spending money?

Here are some practical suggestions which I personally feel conform to biblical principles:

1. *Christians must budget their finances so God comes first.* We should set aside, in cash, a certain percentage of our weekly or monthly income for God. And we must keep complete and accurate records, because if we don't, we may overspend in certain areas and we'll end up spending what we had hoped to give to the Lord's work. At this point, it's very easy to rationalize because the Scriptures are very clear that we should "owe nothing to anyone." The Lord, of course, to whom we owe everything, comes out on the short end.

2. *Whenever possible, we should pay cash for purchases.* There are exceptions, of course, such as people who have expense accounts that are regularly and systematically paid out of reserves set aside for this purpose. It is also necessary in our culture to have several credit cards in order to establish good credit ratings and to have them available for emergency situations. But it is a good rule to never use these cards unless it is an emergency or part of an overall financial plan that is carefully controlled.

3. *Avoid borrowing money and making purchases involving long-term payments and interest rates.* Exceptions, of course, are purchasing a home, an automobile, or in some instances, establishing a solid business venture. And eventually, it is a better stewardship plan to try to get to the place where you can pay cash for an automobile. In so doing you'll earn interest on the money you're saving for the purchase if you deposit it in a savings account, and you'll avoid paying interest on the purchase. This, of course, is not possible for most

people who are just beginning to establish their own financial independence.

4. *If necessary, seek advice on how to set up a monthly budget so you don't spend money recklessly, without a financial frame of reference.* We must be aware at all times if we are overspending in certain areas in relationship to our income and our specific needs.

5. *We should seek advice from both Christian and non-Christian experts regarding financial planning.* We should seek help from several viewpoints. Christians *are* responsible to provide for their families in case of death. But again, we must maintain a unique balance between trusting God and having a sound approach to insurance and investments.

6. *Make sure you have a legally drawn will in the state in which you live.* This is of the utmost importance because of the complicated procedures in the American courts.

LIFE RESPONSE

Use the above suggestions as a checklist for your own life-style. Though you may not agree with every idea, what are your alternatives in light of the biblical principles we've studied? Check those items where you need to take action and then proceed to act on your decision.

FAMILY OR GROUP PROJECT

Discuss with your spouse the ideas suggested in this chapter. What do you feel are weaknesses in your financial philosophy? If necessary, take action to correct any problems in your approach to spending money. Then discuss with your family what your decisions are.

Note to singles: Now is the time to begin firming up your financial philosophy and plans. Don't wait until you are married to begin being a good steward for Jesus Christ.

14

ABRAHAM'S PILGRIMAGE IN PERSPECTIVE

But seek first His kingdom, and His righteousness; and all these things shall be added to you.

Matthew 6:33

As we approach the end of Abraham's life, which in all spanned a period of 175 years (Gen. 25:7), there is no doubt that we have observed a man whose supreme desire was to know God personally, to obey all His commands, to walk in His will. His life-style stands out on the pages of Scripture as one of the most exemplary of the Old Testament characters.

Emerging from raw paganism, Abraham became one of God's most faithful servants. His mistakes are just as obvious as his successes, but his overall progress was always onward and upward. As the writer of the Hebrew letter noted, Abraham's weaknesses faded into the background in the light of his strengths. "By faith Abraham, when he was called, obeyed by going out to a place which he was to receive for an inheritance; and he went out, not knowing where he was going. By faith he lived as an alien in the land of promise, as in a foreign land, dwelling in tents ... for he was looking for the city which has foundations, whose architect and builder is God" (Heb. 11:8–10).

Abraham's life-style was characterized by two distinct, but overlapping, perspectives. First, *he knew this earth was not his real home.* And second, *his eyes were always directed heavenward.*

ABRAHAM'S PERSPECTIVE ON LIFE
IN THIS WORLD (Heb. 11:9)

This Old Testament saint lived "as an alien in the land of promise." To him it was a foreign land. Though it was a land promised to him, somehow he recognized his temporary status. Thus he did not settle permanently in any particular location. He was the first of the pilgrim fathers.

Abraham's dwelling place emerges as a symbol of his life-style and the spirit that pervaded his soul. He left Haran at age 75 and died at age 175. For a century he wandered about the land living in tents.

Abraham was always a friend and a witness to his neighbors, yet he did not engage in their pagan activities. As the father of all of us who believe, he set the example of separation without isolation. He was in the world but not of the world. He lived among his pagan friends, but was not one with them. He avoided their immoral revelries and their pagan rites.

When Sarah died at age 127, Abraham insisted on paying full market value for her burial place, even though Ephron, the son of Zohar, respected him so highly he wanted to give him the cave of Machpelah free of charge. But Abraham refused the gift. He wanted no obligation to anyone but to his God (Gen. 23).

Later yet, when Abraham considered the need for a wife for Isaac, he sent his faithful servant back to his own country to look among his relatives for a girl who believed in the One True God (Gen. 24). Abraham knew that intermarriage with nonbelievers was a violation of the will of God.

Abraham, then, was a stranger and a sojourner in the land of Canaan (Gen. 23:4). He was ever on the move. His dwelling place could be dismantled and quickly erected in another place within a matter of hours.

How easy it would have been for this wealthy Old Testament saint to purchase a choice piece of property, build a huge and permanent mansion, and settle down. Actually, he had the wealth and the manpower to build a castle (Gen. 24:35).

Or how tempting it must have been on occasions to want to return to the lush pasturelands in the Mesopotamian valley, the beautiful and secure land of his childhood. There was certainly "opportunity to return," but he did not (Heb. 11:15).

Why?

Because Abraham was bent on doing the will of God. God had called him to leave his homeland and, though he did not understand all that God was accomplishing through his life and all that He would accomplish through those who lived after him, he walked in the light he had and obeyed what God had revealed. Even though he "died in faith, without receiving the promises" (Heb. 11:13), he seemingly never doubted the promise. He was a man of faith. He believed God!

ABRAHAM'S PERSPECTIVE ON LIFE IN THE WORLD TO COME (Heb. 11:10)

For Abraham, there was something beyond his life on earth that was far more important than a permanent dwelling place. "He was looking for the city which has foundations, whose architect and builder is God" (Heb. 11:10). Though his understanding was limited, Abra-

158

ham knew in his heart that what really counts lies in the realm of the spirit. Thus he was looking for "a better country," "a heavenly one" (Heb. 11:16).

Just as Abraham's *tent* served as a symbol of his view of material possessions, so another symbol stands out boldly during his sojourn in Canaan to reflect his spiritual perspective. Everywhere he pitched his tent, he built an *altar* to the Lord. There he worshiped God. And there he taught "his children and his household" to love God and to learn to do His will (see Gen. 18:19).

Abraham, like all of us, lived in a world of people and things. And like men throughout the centuries, Abraham could have easily lost sight of God and the place He wanted in his life. This is why Moses warned the children of Israel so specifically against the dangers of materialism as they were about to enter the Promised Land.

Listen to his words of caution: "For the Lord your God is bringing you into a good land, a land of brooks of water, of fountains and springs, flowing forth in valleys and hills; a land of wheat and barley, of vines and fig trees and pomegranates, a land of olive oil and honey; a land where you shall eat food without scarcity, in which you shall not lack anything; a land whose stones are iron, and out of whose hills you can dig copper. When you have eaten and are satisfied, you shall bless the Lord your God for the good land which He has given you.

"Beware lest you forget the Lord your God by not keeping His commandments and His ordinances and His statutes which I am commanding you today; lest, when you have eaten and are satisfied, and have built good houses and lived in them, and when your herds and your flocks multiply, and your silver and gold multiply, and all that you have multiplies, then your heart becomes proud, and you forget the Lord your God who brought you out from the land of Egypt, out of the house of slavery" (Deut. 8:7–14).

The tragedy, of course, is that the children of Israel did forget God. They became materialists. Eventually they did the very thing Moses warned them about when he said: "You may say in your heart, 'My power and the strength of my hand made me this wealth'" (Deut. 8: 17). Rather than worshiping the God who gave them all of their earthly possessions, they began to worship the possessions themselves. When they did, they ceased walking in the will of God.

Abraham's perspectives were never blurred and out of focus. Though he made mistakes, he never lost sight of God's promise—of God's plan, and most important, he did not lose sight of God Himself. He worshiped Him and demonstrated his dedication by being willing to sacrifice his very son to please the One who had called him out of the land of Ur.

A NEW TESTAMENT PERSPECTIVE

Being an alien and a stranger on earth is not just an Old Testament concept experienced exclusively by great men like Abraham, Isaac, Jacob and David. In fact, it is only as we gain a New Testament perspective that we can fully grasp the real meaning of what it means to be a pilgrim. Listen to the words of various apostles as they corresponded with different groups of New Testament Christians, instructing them regarding the very perspectives that were so exemplary in the life of Abraham.

1. The Corinthian Christians: *"We have a house not made with hands."*

"Therefore we do not lose heart, but though our outer man is decaying, yet our inner man is being renewed day by day. For momentary, light affliction is producing for us an eternal weight of glory far beyond all comparison, while we look not at the things which are seen, but at the things which are not seen; for the things which are seen are temporal, but the things which are not seen are eternal. For we know that if the earthly tent which is our house is torn down, we have a building from God, *a house not made with hands*, eternal in the heavens" (2 Cor. 4:16—5:1, italics added).

The "house" or "tent" to which Paul refers is our earthly body. Our bodies are deteriorating. The bodies of Paul and some of his fellow missionaries deteriorated more rapidly than they should have because of severe physical and psychological persecution. But their motivation and desire to keep doing God's will were directly related to their earthly and heavenly perspectives. They knew that to experience death meant life—an endless existence and a new "house not made with hands," a new body (see 1 Cor. 15:51–54).

2. The Philippian Christians: *"Our citizenship is in heaven."*

"Brethren, join in following my example, and observe those who walk according to the pattern you have in us. For many walk, of whom I often told you, and now tell you even weeping, that they are enemies of the cross of Christ, whose end is destruction, whose god is their appetite, and whose glory is in their shame, who set their minds on earthly things. For *our citizenship is in heaven*, from which also we eagerly wait for a Savior, the Lord Jesus Christ; who will transform the body of our humble state into conformity with the body of His glory, by the exertion of the power that He has even to subject all things to Himself" (Phil. 3:17–21, italics added).

A Christian's true citizenship is not on earth. It is in heaven. Abraham knew this. And so did other Old Testament saints who had a correct perspective on life. They, like New Testament Christians who also had a correct perspective, stood out in bold contrast to those who were worshiping the gods of this world. Paul names those gods for the Philippian Christians—the gods of self-gratification, lust, sin and any other earthly thing that is more important than the true God of heaven.

3. The scattered Christians: *"We are aliens and strangers."*

"Peter, an apostle of Jesus Christ, to those who reside as aliens. . . . But you are a chosen race, a royal priesthood, a holy nation, a people for God's own possession, that you may proclaim the excellencies of Him who has called you out of darkness into His marvelous light; for once you were not a people, but now you are the people of God; you had not received mercy, but now you have received mercy. Beloved, I urge you as *aliens and strangers* to abstain from fleshly lusts, which wage war against the soul" (1 Pet. 1:1; 2:9–11, italics added).

Here Peter uses the same words which describe Abraham's life-style. The New Testament Christians are *aliens* and *strangers*. And because of this unique citizenship which is in heaven, they are to focus on their position in Christ, not their position on earth. Like true pilgrims, they are to "abstain from fleshly lusts, which wage war against the soul" and to keep their "behavior excellent among" those who are yet only citizens on this earth (1 Pet. 2:12).

4. The Hebrew Christians: *"We are seeking the city which is to come."*

"For here we do not have a lasting city, but *we are seeking the city which is to come.* Through Him then let us continually offer up a sacrifice of praise to God, that is, the fruit of lips that give thanks to His name. And do not neglect doing good and sharing; for with such sacrifices God is pleased" (Heb. 13:14–16, italics added).

I've purposely treated this passage last because it is an extension of the concept the Hebrew author developed in Hebrews 11 when talking about Abraham's life-style.

Like this Old Testament saint, the Hebrew Christians didn't have "a lasting city" on this earth. Consequently, they too were to keep their eyes focused on "the city which is to come."

And how were they to do that?

They, too, were to offer sacrifices, not animals slain on a primitive altar, but a "sacrifice of praise to God, that is, the fruit of lips that give thanks to His name." And further, their material possessions were to be a means, not only to meet their own needs, but the needs of others. They were not to "neglect doing good and sharing," said the Hebrew writer, "for with such sacrifices God is pleased." New Testament Christians, then, must worship God with their lips and their lives; with their words and their works; with their voices and their vocations; and with their praise and their possessions.

A TWENTIETH-CENTURY PERSPECTIVE

Believers living in the twentieth century, particularly Americans, have difficulty identifying with New Testament Christians. Many of us know little or nothing of their persecutions, of their pain, of their poverty. Many first-century believers could grab hold more easily of what it really meant to be a stranger on earth and a citizen of heaven, for in reality they had only their heavenly citizenship. They were often disowned, many were slaves, and many lost everything they possessed on this earth because of their commitment to Jesus Christ.

How should twentieth-century Christians—particularly those of us who are blessed abundantly with health, a house, a lovely family and financial security—how can we develop a biblical perspective on life in this world? How can we live as strangers and foreigners and pilgrims on this earth? Do we have to be poor to be committed Christians?

Not at all! Though, let's face reality. The more a man

has of this world's goods, the greater his temptation to forget about God. The children of Israel are a dramatic example of this process.

Jesus Christ often warned people against the dangers inherent in riches. Said He: "Do not lay up for yourselves treasures upon earth, where moth and rust destroy, and where thieves break in and steal; but lay up for yourselves treasures in heaven, where neither moth nor rust destroys, and where thieves do not break in or steal; for where your treasure is, there will your heart be also" (Matt. 6:19–21).

Listen also to the apostle Paul: "But those who want to get rich fall into temptation and a snare and many foolish and harmful desires which plunge men into ruin and destruction. For the love of money is a root of all sorts of evil, and some by longing for it have wandered away from the faith, and pierced themselves with many a pang" (1 Tim. 6:9,10).

Though those who accumulate much of this world's possessions are more vulnerable to Satan's attacks, these people can still have a correct perspective on God and the life to come. This was true of Abraham, for much of his life he was greatly blessed with material possessions. His pagan neighbors classified him as a "mighty prince" (Gen. 23:6). And his servant, who journeyed back to Abraham's homeland to find a wife for Isaac, paid this outstanding tribute to his master—"I am Abraham's servant. And the Lord has greatly blessed my master, so that he has become rich; and He has given him flocks and herds, and silver and gold, and servants and maids, and camels and donkeys" (Gen. 24:34,35). Yet with all of this, Abraham throughout his life kept a proper perspective. God was first in his life!

So whether a Christian has little or much, whether he is persecuted or promoted, whether he is weak or strong, whether he lives in the first century or the twentieth—it is possible for him to say with Paul, "For to me, to live is Christ" (Phil. 1:21).

But let's be more specific. What must a man *do* to be this kind of man? The Hebrew writer makes it very clear how Christians are to live. If we are to keep our eyes focused on "the city which is to come" we must do two things, the same things Abraham did.

First, *we must continually worship God*, offering "up a sacrifice of praise to God, that is, the fruit of lips that give thanks to His name" (Heb. 13:15).

Second, *we must "not neglect doing good and sharing"* (Heb. 13:16), using our time and our material possessions to minister to other members of the body of Christ and to further the work of God.

These two *actions* will help us keep a proper perspective on life in this world. And don't be deceived. These aspects of life are measurable. We can say we have an attitude of thanksgiving and generosity, but it can only be measured by what we actually do. And once we stop "doing," we are in danger of becoming self-centered materialists, people who find their security in themselves and in the things of this world.

LIFE RESPONSE

To assist you in evaluating your perspective as a Christian, think about the answers to the following questions:

1. *How often do I lift my voice in true praise to God, thanking Him for my blessings in life?* Am I truly thankful, or am I merely mouthing words of ritual?

Note: A true test of our deeper motives and attitude toward God is reflected in how quickly we murmur and complain when things don't go quite our way.

Take a moment now to let your heart flow out to God, first in confession for any ungrateful attitude and action; and second, in thanksgiving and praise to God for the

165

many blessings He has brought into your life. You may not be rich in the things of this world, but have you thanked Him lately for your riches in Christ Jesus?

2. *How am I using my time and material possessions to serve the body of Jesus Christ?* Do I allow my usage of time and money to be dictated by the fast-moving world, by inflation, by competition, by personal desires? Do I focus on myself, putting God second, if not last? Do I *plan* to put God and others first?

Note: Here is a general rule: Unless we are experiencing some personal inconvenience because of the way we use our time and our material possessions, chances are we are not really making much of a sacrifice. And the sacrifice is what is pleasing to God.

Take a moment now to reflect on your program of stewardship. How faithful are you?

Remember: How you use your time and your material possessions is the greatest test of your commitment to Jesus Christ and your desire to do His will. That is why Jesus said: "But seek first His kingdom, and His righteousness; and all these things shall be added to you" (Matt. 6:33).

FAMILY OR GROUP PROJECT

Review this chapter. Read again the passages of 2 Corinthians, Philippians, 1 Peter and Hebrews. Then together evaluate your personal (and group) life-style.

Do you have a correct perspective on life in this world?

THE BIBLICAL RENEWAL SERIES
by
Gene A. Getz

ONE ANOTHER SERIES

Building Up One Another
Encouraging One Another
Loving One Another
Praying for One Another
Serving One Another

PERSONALITY SERIES

When You're Confused and Uncertain (Abraham)
From Prison to Palace (Joseph)
A Man of Prayer (Nehemiah)
Defeat to Victory (Joshua)
When You Feel Like a Failure (David)
When the Pressure's On (Elijah)
When You Feel You Haven't Got It (Moses)

THE MEASURE OF SERIES

Measure of a . . .
    Church
    Family
    Man
    Marriage
    Woman

BIBLE BOOK SERIES

Pressing on When You'd Rather Turn Back
(Philippians)
Saying No When You'd Rather Say Yes
(Titus)
Believing God When You Are Tempted to Doubt
(James 1)
Doing Your Part When You'd Rather Let God Do It All
(James 2-5)
Looking Up When You Feel Down
(Ephesians 1-3)
Living for Others When You'd Rather Live
for Yourself (Ephesians 4-6)
Standing Firm When You'd Rather Retreat
(1 Thessalonians)

Sharpening the Focus of the Church presents an overall
perspective for Church Renewal. All of these books are
available from your bookstore.